A SEPARATE PEACE

NOTES

including
- *Introduction*
- *Chapter Summaries and Commentaries*
- *Character Sketches*
- *Critical Notes*
- *Questions*

by
Cary M. Roberts
University of Mississippi

Cliffs Notes
INCORPORATED
LINCOLN, NEBRASKA 68501

Editor	Consulting Editor
Gary Carey, M.A.	*James L. Roberts, Ph.D.*
University of Colorado	*Department of English*
	University of Nebraska

ISBN 0-8220-1183-2
© Copyright 1965
by
Cliffs Notes, Inc.
All Rights Reserved
Printed in U.S.A.

1996 Printing

Cliffs Notes, Inc.   Lincoln, Nebraska

CONTENTS

A NOTE ON THE AUTHOR

John Knowles was thrust upon the literary scene when his first novel, *A Separate Peace*, won both the Rosenthal Award of the National Institute of Arts and Letters and the William Faulkner Foundation Award. Since then he has published two other novels which have received mixed critical reviews.

Knowles was born on September 16, 1926, in Fairmont, West Virginia. In his fifteenth year, he entered Phillips Exeter Academy and was there during the four years of the Second World War (1941-45). It is highly possible that some of the experiences utilized in *A Separate Peace* took place at this private school. After graduation, Knowles entered Yale University, from which he received a B.A. degree in 1949. While a student at Yale, he edited the *Yale Daily News* and contributed stories to the undergraduate literary magazine.

After leaving Yale, Knowles worked for a while on a newspaper in Connecticut and then accepted a position as an associate editor of the *Holiday* magazines, where he published articles on varying subjects. He soon decided to devote his entire time to writing and traveling. Since his twenty-fifth year, he has lived in France, Italy, the Near East, and the Greek Islands. Of his first novel, Knowles once wrote: "If anything as I wrote tempted me to insert artificial complexities, I ignored it. If anything appeared which looked suspiciously like a symbol, I left it on its own. I thought that if I wrote truly and deeply enough about certain specific people in a certain place at a particular time having certain specific experiences, then the result would be relevant for many other kinds of people and places and times and experiences."

INTRODUCTION

A Separate Peace is a novel involving an adolescent's attempt to understand his world and himself. It is an age-old conflict set against a greater conflict—World War II. In times of peace, the change from adolescence to maturity is in itself a tremendous conflict, but in times of war, the change becomes even more significant because the values of the world and of society are rapidly changing. Gene Forrester, the narrator of the story, is fighting a war within himself, concerning whether to live in the secluded and safe values found in a peaceful prep school or whether to move out of this security and into the confusion of the adult world. At the same time he is waging war against the encroaching domination of his best friend's anarchic approach to life. The novel chronicles Gene's fluctuations between accepting and rejecting diverse aspects of these two worlds.

There are so many opposing elements in the novel that it would be tenuous to relate all of them in a short introduction. Some would include the private war versus the public war; Gene Forrester's view of life versus Finny's view of life; adulthood versus adolescence; and a life of conformity as opposed to a life of freedom and spontaneity. Various aspects of these larger ideas are represented in symbolic form throughout the novel. For example, there is the upper, or clean, Devon River in contrast with the lower, or dirty, Naguamsett River; there is the summer session as opposed to the regular term; there is the life of study as opposed to the life of play; and then there are all the contrasts between time present and time past.

Throughout the novel, one symbol pervades the entire work. This is the tree. Knowles never makes the tree into a symbol which intrudes upon our realistic enjoyment of the novel, but we are constantly aware that it is being used as some sort of symbol. It first becomes a challenge for the boys in the lower grade to overcome. It suggests a victory over fear. But this is the forbidden tree which then suggests the biblical tree of knowledge or the tree of forbidden fruit. Using this view, we see that Gene becomes a changed person after jumping from the tree. Furthermore, he later uses the tree as the instrument by which he maims his best friend. In general, therefore, each reader should be aware of the varying ways in which the author uses the tree as a symbol and should be prepared to react to differing interpretations concerning its symbolic importance.

LIST OF CHARACTERS

Gene Forrester

The narrator, who tells of his prep school experiences during his sixteenth and seventeenth years.

Phineas (Finny)

Gene's roommate and best friend, the best athlete in the school.

Brinker Hadley

One of the students, a leader of the class and the instigator of a trial against Gene.

Leper (Elwin Lepellier)

Another student, who becomes the first from the school to enlist in the armed service. He later becomes the first casualty when he "cracks up."

Chet Douglass, Bobby Zane, and Quackenbush

Additional students who function only in minor roles.

Mr. Prud'homme, Mr. Patch-Withers, and Mr. Ludsbury
Teachers at Devon School.

Dr. Stanpole
The doctor who treats Finny's leg.

GENERAL PLOT SUMMARY

Returning to Devon School, Gene Forrester remembers his experiences there during the summer session when he was sixteen years old. The Second World War had just begun then. He remembers that his friend and roommate, Phineas (Finny) was considered the best athlete in the school and that one afternoon they went to a large tree by the river. Phineas suggested that they jump from this tree and land in the river beneath them. It was the first time that anyone so young had tried this feat usually reserved for older boys. Both successfully made the jump even though Gene was frightened. After this first jump, Finny organizes the Summer Suicide Society, which devotes itself to initiating members by having them jump from the tree into the river. Each time, he and Gene must make the first jump, but Gene never loses his fear of jumping.

Finny was considered the best athlete in school, and Gene tried to compensate by being the best student in school. After a few weeks of joining all of Finny's activities, Gene thinks that Finny is intentionally trying to make him fail out of school. He begins to resent Finny's many and involved activities. This resentment builds in Gene's mind until at the end of the summer, with many tests approaching, Gene must interrupt his studies too often to go jump from the tree. Finally, on one occasion, he impulsively jounces the limb and Finny falls.

Gene hears from the doctor that Finny's leg is so shattered that he can never again play any sport and will be lucky to walk again. Gene fears that Finny will report that he was pushed off the limb, but on his first visit to the infirmary, Gene knows that Finny has removed all suspicion from his mind. He trusts Gene completely and would never think of accusing Gene.

After the summer vacation, Gene detours by Finny's home and here decides to confess to Finny that he had pushed him out of the tree. But Finny refuses to believe the confession and makes Gene leave. Back at school, everything is different without Phineas. Gene doesn't even bother to go out for any of the sports.

In the dormitory, a schoolmate jokingly teases that Gene deliberately "did away" with Finny so that Gene could have a room all to himself. Gene doesn't like the joke but feels that he has to go along with it.

The autumn session is also different because the students volunteer to do jobs left vacant because the workers are off to the war. Once, when many students have finished shoveling snow from a blocked railroad, many of them decide to enlist immediately. Gene is going to follow suit until he returns to his room and finds that Finny has returned to school. Then all thoughts of war fade from his mind.

Finny tells Gene that he must now develop into a good athlete for both of them. Finny will coach Gene for the 1944 Olympics. Gene tries to explain that with the war, sports are no longer important, but Finny refuses to believe in the war. He feels he has more insights than most people because he has now suffered so much. Soon, Gene begins to lapse into Finny's world of peace. A friend's enlistment does not even bring the war close to Gene. And later when the friend "cracks up" Gene goes to see him but still refuses to allow his friend's problems to intrude upon his present life.

Some time later, some of the boys from the dormitory come to get Gene and Finny. They all go to a big assembly room, where they want to clear up the matter of Finny's broken leg. They begin asking questions and suddenly, Gene realizes that he is being accused. Finny refuses to answer all the questions; he has put aside the possibility of Gene's guilt. He leaves the room in a terribly agitated state and falls on the slippery stairs and breaks the same leg again.

Gene follows Finny to the infirmary and tries to see him but this time Finny will not have anything to do with Gene. The next day, Finny wants to know why Gene pushed him out of the tree. It is agreed that the act was some sort of blind impulse. Later in the day when the doctor is resetting Finny's leg, some of the marrow gets into the bloodstream and Finny dies instantly. Gene does not cry then or ever about the death of his friend because he feels that he too has died and one doesn't cry over one's own death.

Later Gene realizes that the war never meant anything to him because he had fought his own private war and that he had killed his enemy at the school.

SUMMARIES AND COMMENTARIES

CHAPTER 1

Summary

The narrator, Gene Forrester, returns to Devon School, where he was a student some fifteen years earlier. The school seems the same as far as the buildings are concerned, but fifteen years ago, there was a war going on.

As he walks about the campus, Gene realizes that he lived in great fear while he was a student. But he had not been able to identify his fear because it was always present. He has come back specifically to visit two fearful spots. One is the First Building (so named because it had been burnt and rebuilt and was still the main building) and the other is a tree down by the river. After noticing that the building is essentially the same as when he was there, Gene walks across the campus toward the river. It is a rainy day and he has to walk through a lot of mud in order to get to the river.

At first, he cannot recognize the tree that he is searching for. There are so many more than he has remembered. Then he finds one with "certain small scars rising along its trunk" and with one limb "extending over the river." This was the tree, but it is changed from what he remembers. He realizes that "nothing endures, not a tree, not love, not even a death by violence."

Walking away, he remembers his sixteenth year when he was an "Upper Middler" at Devon. He and Phineas (Finny) and three others come to look at the tree. Finny thinks it would be a "cinch" to jump from the limb into the water. Standing on a limb, "you could by a prodigious effort jump far enough out into the river for safety." But no Upper Middler has ever tried it. Finny is going to be the first.

Finny doesn't bother to talk about jumping; he simply asks who wants to be first. He is considered the best athlete in Devon, but Gene notes that he does not have an exceptional build. No one answers Finny, so he scrambles up the tree. Shouting about his contribution to the war, he jumps and falls "through the tips of some lower branches, and...into the water." Coming out, he says that the jump was the most fun he has had in a week. He asks "Who's next?" Suddenly, Gene finds that he is taking off his clothes and is up on the limb. He has no intention of jumping that day, but somehow Finny has gotten a hold over him; there he is, about to jump.

With a sensation that he is throwing his life away, he jumps and lands in the water. He feels fine. Finny tries to get the others to jump, but they adamantly refuse. He turns to Gene and says, "It's...just you and me."

Walking back to the dormitory, Finny tries to kid Gene about how he was shamed into jumping. Gene denies it and they playfully wrestle several times. Each time, Finny wins. The others urge Finny and Gene to hurry because they will be late for supper. Surprisingly Gene resents the dinner bell and the conformity, and even though he realizes that Finny trapped him into becoming his collaborator, he jumps on Finny for another bout of wrestling, thinking that this will make them miss their dinner. This is what Finny wanted. When they are sure that they have missed dinner, they quit and return to the dormitory. They read their assignments and go to bed.

Commentary

The first paragraph lets us know that the story is going back into the past. Consequently, we must be constantly alert to determine what this return to the past means in light of the later narration. The return to events in Gene's sixteenth and seventeeth years prepare us for an initiation story, that is, a story in which a young boy is initiated into certain aspects of life. Thus, we must observe each incident to see what the narrator will learn from this particular event. Furthermore, we must be aware that the events of the past are narrated against the background of the Second World War. To complement this, we have the more personal war being fought between Finny and Gene, but this second war is staged almost entirely within the mind of the narrator. There are also intrusions of a third war based on the school's intense athletic rivalry.

The difference between the past of fifteen years ago and the present can be seen in many of the descriptions. For example, the school now looks like a museum to the narrator, but earlier when he was there it "was vibrantly real." Thus, by these suggestions, we realize that Gene, the narrator, has learned a great deal about himself. This idea is further emphasized then the narrator notes that he lived in great fear during the past, but nevertheless did not understand this fear. Now after the lapse of time, he is able to evaluate the influence this fear had upon his life. In other words, he has matured and has incorporated the experiences of his youth into his total system of values. Some would then ask if this is so, why then does he return. In terms of the narrative, Gene returns simply to compare his emotional status with what it was fifteen years earlier.

It is important to note that the narrator visits two places when he re-turns. We later learn that these are the two areas which have most influ-enced his life. He first goes to the academic building (sometimes called the Main Hall and most often the First Building) because it was here that Phineas and Gene were brought before the group of students in order to be examined for the accident involving Finny's leg. Furthermore, it was in this building that Finny broke his leg for the second time. The second place he visits is the tree by the river. Gene pushed Finny from the tree and broke his leg the first time. Thus, the narrator is still noting "how far [his] convalescence had gone" as concerns his emotional maturity.

When the narrator leaves the First Building and goes toward the river, he must trudge through some soft and muddy ground which was "dooming his city shoes." He feels that at any other time, he would "have felt like a fool slogging through mud and rain, only to look at a tree." The mud that he plows through is somewhat symbolic. When Gene first jumps from the tree, he lands in the soft mud at the bottom of the river. Thus, his trudging through the mud here suggests a return to elemental emotions and elemental fears. The rain is also symbolic and — as will be noted throughout the novel — rain and water play an important symbolic role in Gene's life.

When he arrives at the river, he observes that there is a fog hanging over it, which obscures his vision. He cannot see so clearly the things which were so important to him as a youth. Likewise, there is a change in the physical appearance of the tree. This suggests the change which has taken place in the narrator, in fact the change that takes place in all man-kind and throughout all time. Gene finally identifies the tree by the "small scars rising along its trunk" and seems to think that some of these scars are those left by his youth. still showing faintly on the adult man. Further-more, he realizes that everything has changed: "Nothing endures, not a tree, not love not even a death by violence." Realizing this, he heads back through the mud and the heavy rain.

At this point, we have an immediate return to the past and the first thing introduced is the "all-important" tree. The reader should note, how-ever, that the tree is merely introduced. Knowles does not linger in de-scribing it or in attaching heavy symbolic importance to it, even though this tree does assume immense importance later in the work. In the three short sentences describing the tree, he packs into this description three heavily charged religious terms — *steeple*, *damned*, and *hell* — suggesting that if Gene climbs the tree (or steeple) he will be damned to a hell of envy and confused values. Phineas is also deftly described through off-hand colloquialisms – some of these include words like *crazy, hypnotist, maniac, droll,* and *goofy*. These terms suggest that Finny will not be classified as among the ordinary students. Through the use of this type of language, we are able to subtly discern that Finny is removed from the average run-of-the-mill student. Furthermore, Finny's first comment characterizes him. He observes the tree and says, "What I like best about this tree...is that it's such a cinch." Actually, the tree is anything but a cinch, hence making the statement ironic, but Finny is always saying and doing the unexpected. We should also remember that this "cinch" of a tree will be the instrument of Finny's crippling, thereby making the statement doubly ironic.

Knowles is the master of understatement. For example, in describing Finny's early actions, Gene mentions that Finny always said "aey-uh" and that this "weird New England affirmative...always made me laugh, as Finny knew, so I had to laugh." It will be developed as a part of Finny's nature that he often sets up some situation in which he knows all the terms or in which he is the master of the events. His greatest pleasure, however, is having a surprise pulled on him in which he is not the master of the situation. At the end of the chapter, Gene trips Finny by surprise and Finny is delighted with this little trick.

Almost unknowing Gene begins to make Finny into some type of demigod who should be worshiped. Finny becomes some type of ideal who never makes a blunder or mistake. He is described as moving with perfect physical grace and harmony. But at the same time, Gene points out that he and Finny are the same size and that neither of them was of exceptional height or physical build. Thus, in comparison we must realize that Finny gains his power and influence through personal magnetism and not from any ready-made status acquired from the possession of a large physique.

Finny's physical attributes receive more attention in terms of his harmonious movement, his ability to flow rather than walk, his perfect coordination. Gene's life has been one of conformity, of moving with a received tradition. Ironically, Finny's influence in Gene's life will be in the nature of interference with natural impulses of conformity, of making Gene do the unexpected, such as jumping from the tree or later going to the beach and failing tests. Consequently, even early in this first chapter, Gene seems to realize that Finny is getting "some kind of hold over" him. This hold Finny has on Gene will become the central conflict of the novel and will influence many of Gene's actions. He will fluctuate between extreme like and dislike of his position.

The central dramatic episode of the first chapter is the jump from the tree. It is superfluous here to attempt to give all the symbolism connected with the tree itself. It is enough to say that the jump from the tree becomes a means of rejecting a certain aspect of his past life. Gene feels that when he jumped there was "the sensation that I was throwing my life away." In one sense he is throwing all of his conformity and continuity of the past away and is entering into a new life. It is as though he is symbolically baptized by the river beneath him. When he does emerge and begins his return to the dormitory, he "resented the bell and my West Point stride and hurrying and conforming." He realizes that Finny was right. Thus again, Gene is breaking with one aspect of the past and with one aspect of his own character and is attempting to absorb a part of Finny's more free and erratic nature. He begins to accept Finny's view that "authority [was] the necessary evil against which happiness [is] achieved by reaction." Previously, Gene was a person who always obeyed rules, and later when Finny is confined to Boston with his broken leg, Gene returns to an absolute allegiance to authority. We will see that Gene can only rebel against authority when he has the moral support offered by Finny.

Once other aspect of Finny's nature is given at the end of the chapter. Finny is a strange character of reversals which Gene cannot understand. Gene seems to desire consistency in actions and Finny is always reversing himself. For example, at the end of the chapter, Finny refuses to wear pajamas because he has heard that they are unmilitary. Yet later, Finny refuses to believe in the war and still later we hear that Finny wrote every branch of service, both American and foreign, trying to get accepted. Even the game invented by Finny — blitzball — involves in its strategy types of sudden reversals. In other words, Finny responds to the moment, whereas Gene will try to give consistency and continuity to his life.

CHAPTER 2

Summary

Mr. Prud'homme, one of the substitute teachers for the summer session, stops by to question Gene and Finny about missing dinner. Finny begins immediately to give him a "scatterbrained" explanation about the necessity of jumping out of the tree because everyone has to prepare for the war. Mr. Prud'homme listens with amazement but also with friendliness. Finny presses his advantage because "unregulated friendliness [is] one of Finny's reasons for living."

The rules, however, are rather lax during the summer term. It is almost as though the students reminded the faculty of "what peace was like" when one is "sixteen, careless and wild." "Phineas was the essence of this careless peace." One day he decides to wear a very pink shirt which will be his emblem because there was no flag nor an "Old Glory" that they could display. No one but Finney would have dared wear such a shirt. When one of the masters questions him about the shirt, Finny gives such a fantastic answer that Gene realizes "Phineas could get away with any-thing." He is beginning to envy his friend.

That afternoon, Mr. Patch-Withers gives the traditional term tea, and Phineas wears his pink shirt. He talks constantly and spontaneously to the entire group, expressing his opinions about the recent bombings and other matters. He enjoys himself so much that he unbuttons his jacket. Everyone gasps when Mrs. Patch-Withers notices that Phineas is wearing the official Devon School tie as a belt. Gene feels "unexpectedly excited" over the fact that Phineas would not be able "to get away with it." But Phineas gives a wild, fanciful explanation that his tie and shirt all "tie in together" with the bombing of Central Europe. Mr. Patch-Withers thinks it is the "strangest tribute" to the school, but he seems pleased. So Phineas gets away with even this.

After he finishes his explanation, Finny adds that he wouldn't have wanted his pants to fall down at the official tea. Even old, sour Mr. Patch-Withers breaks into a laugh, and Gene feels a "sudden stab of disappoint-ment" because Phineas *was* going to get away with it. "He got away with everything because of the extraordinary kind of person he was."

After the party, Phineas suggests that they need to clear their heads of all the talk, even though he has done most of the talking. As they walk to-ward the river, Finny says he doesn't really believe that "we bombed Cen-tral Europe." Gene agrees with him. When they arrive at the river, Phineas wonders if Gene is still afraid to jump. Gene tells him it would be a pleasure, but as he climbs the tree, he feels somewhat rigid. Finny feels that they are cementing their friendship by jumping together and suggests that they form a "suicide society." They agree on the name — "The Super Suicide Society of the Summer Session."

As they are climbing out on the limb to jump, suddenly Gene feels a "moment of total, impersonal panic" and loses his balance. Finny reaches out and grabs him. With his balance restored, Gene makes his jump. The "Super Suicide Society" is formed.

That night, Gene realizes that Finny practically saved his life. Other-wise, he would have fallen from the limb and killed himself.

Commentary

The essence of this chapter is devoted to establishing Finny's character and Gene's reaction to Finny's nature. In the meeting with Mr. Prud'homme, we see that Finny offered a scatterbrained explanation for missing a meal. As he talked he noticed that Mr. Prud'homme responded to Finny's explanation. Gene then understands that Finny likes nothing better than "unregulated friendliness." Scenes such as this "were one of Finny's reasons for living." Furthermore, Finny is constantly able to talk himself out of any situation. We begin then to see him as the spontaneous individual who "can get away with anything," even wearing the school tie as a belt to the term tea.

Finny's relaxed and free nature causes Gene some envy and some jealousy. Throughout the chapter and subsequent scenes, Gene is always hoping to see Finny get punished for something. He hopes that Finny will not be able to get away with some of his pranks. In other words, Gene is hoping to see Finny brought down to a human level where it is possible to compete with him. Furthermore, these "sudden stabs of disappointment" on Gene's part are part of the motivation for his pushing Finny out of the tree later on. When Gene thinks that Finny "wasn't going to get away with" the tie episode, he feels himself "becoming unexpectedly excited at that." Only by Finny's failure to accomplish something or failure to get away with something can Gene enter into a rivalry with him. Instead, Finny seems to function almost as a person (or demigod) who stands outside the realm of normal human activity and normal human emotions.

There are many images used in this chapter to indicate aspects of Finny's nature. He is covered with "sunburned health," and he possesses a "scatterbrained eloquence" which he uses both with his peer group and with the masters. It is this quality which will allow him to get by with so much, and later he invents such scatterbrained games as blitzball. Another quality emphasized is Finny's constant desire to be surprised. Finny "might have rather enjoyed the punishment if it was done in some novel and unknown way." Even in perversity, Finny can enjoy a situation if it presents something new and different.

Another important image to note is Gene's use of the word "forbidden" in connection with the tree. It recalls immediately the forbidden tree in the Garden of Eden. On the contrary, Finny refers to the jump as one of those things that the boys naturally had to do. It is the most unnatural thing for Gene, yet for Finny it is a natural thing for a young boy to do. This again suggests the opposing natures of the two boys.

Finny's explanation of why he jumped from the tree involves his belief that "we are all getting ready for the war." But for the masters Finny is the "essence of this careless peace." Consequently, the masters see Finny as possessing all the qualities that the free and careless young man should possess, but in actuality, Finny has not forgotten the war. In fact, part of his nature is this ironic contradiction. In terms of the entire book, we know that no person at Devon is more concerned with the war than is Finny, but at the same time, no person there except Finny pretends to believe that there is no war—but that it is a part of a great hoax. For example, in this chapter, Finny justifies his wearing of the tie because it all ties in with the bombing in Central Europe, after the party is over, he tells Gene that he doesn't believe that the allies really bombed Central Europe. Consequently, Finny's spontaneous and natural ability to evoke the right explanation at the right moment makes him the symbol to the faculty of "the life the war was being fought to preserve."

Finny's reverse or contradictory nature is also suggested in his "calm ignorance of the rules" combined with a "winning urge to be good." He "seemed to love the school truly and deeply, and never more than when he was breaking the regulations." It is this spontaneous and contradictory nature which Gene cannot understand and which ultimantely contributes to his attempting to destroy Finny.

This novel takes as its framework the actual war of the adults, World War II, and this war is set against the mythical peace of the adolescents. When the adults look back on adolescence they see the good years and fail to remember all the struggles. The adult fails to remember that passing from adolescence to maturity is, in itself, a continuing war and battle. This novel then will be a relating of Gene's insights and struggles which lead him to his full maturity.

The book, being about adolescents, deals with the knowns and the unknowns of the world. The world of the child and the adolescent can be seen to be one of unknown expectation. However, that world has changed because of the war, and the adolescent is no longer in the innocent world. The war has brought an end to that innocence. Gene is the example of this, since he has been leading a life of regularity and conformity. Thus, when he jumps from the tree, it is as though Gene is returning to the world of the unknown; he is entering, or trying to enter, into Finny's world.

Finny's world is also somewhat the world of the adolescent. Most of the typical students try to imitate the adult world and dress like the mature man, but Finny rebelliously wears a flaming pink shirt which contradicts the rest of the dress in the school. It is the unexpected thing to wear, and Finny does so as an emblem of the war. His actions then are so paradoxical as to leave poor Gene completely stunned and confused. He wants to enter into Finny's world but cannot bring himself to act with such nonchalance and disregard for established behavior. Finny, however, continues to cut through all the established reactions. He is even described as possessing the "sharp look of a prow," which suggests again how Finny breaks through all established tradition and sets up his own world.

Note that during the term tea Finny delights in putting himself into a dangerous situation, largely because he likes the challenge of getting out of the situation. He goes into an illogical explanation—Gene sees most of Finny's actions as illogical—about his tie and the war effort but then adds that he didn't think of that when he put the tie on. In other words, Finny has gotten out of the scrape, but then refuses to let it alone and puts himself out on another limb by admitting his explanation was unpremeditated. He then saves himself from the second predicament by his use of humor. He says merely that he would not want his pants to fall down at the master's tea. Thus, as with the tree and jumping from the limb, Finny delights in placing himself in difficult positions so that he can get out of them.

For a third time in this chapter Finny has placed himself in a tenuous position. First, it was with Mr. Prud'homme when Finny volunteered to tell about jumping out of the tree and then jusified it as a part of preparing for the war. Second, with Mr. Patch-Withers, Finny admits more than is necessary and gets out of the difficulty. Now after leaving, he admits to Gene that he doesn't believe that the Americans bombed Central Europe. This is like admitting to Gene that everything previously said was a lie. But of course, we know that when Finny said these things, he said them spontaneously and naturally. But when he admits to Gene his belief, it was said "thoughtfully." Note further that Gene here agrees with Finny. In other words, Gene accepts Finny's account without ever contradicting him. It will only be after Finny is wounded that Gene will be able to contradict Finny.

At the end of the chapter, Gene and Finny form a suicide society. Finny wants to call it the *Super* Suicide Society of the Summer Session. The *super* indicates the degree to which Finny wants to carry things. In the normal pastoral school, Finny likes to introduce the strange and, perhaps, destructive element. Certainly for Gene, this society is a destructive element because he is cutting himself off from everything he has believed in. A type of ethical suicide evolves as Gene accepts Finny's views and rejects his own way of life.

A special bond is sealed between Finny and Gene as Finny makes Gene jump first. As they are about to jump, Gene almost loses his balance and is saved by Finny. This scene parallels Finny's later fall, when just before falling, he reaches back for Gene's hand, but Gene has jounced the limb and allows Finny to fall.

After this scene is over, Finny apparently thinks no more about it. Later, however, Gene thinks about it and realizes that he could have been killed and that Finny "had practically saved my life." This realization now is an ironic contrast to what Gene later does to Finny. But also, we should be aware that Gene contemplates these acts and tries to draw significance from them, whereas Finny merely acts without thinking about them.

CHAPTER 3

Summary

Gene realized that Finny had practically saved his life, but that he also practically lost it for him. That is, Gene wouldn't have been in the tree in the first place had it not been for Finny. He concludes that he need not "feel any tremendous rush of gratitude toward Phineas."

The Super Suicide Society is a success from the very first. They begin to meet every night and initiate new members. Every session must open with Gene and Finny making jumps. Gene has never got used to the idea of jumping and hates each time, but he cannot refuse, fearing loss of Finny's respect. Gene is still acting against every instinct of his own nature.

Gene begins to realize that Finny's mind and nature are completely opposite to his. For example, Finny believes "you always win at sports." He refuses to understand that when one side wins, someone else has to lose. In general, Finny is disappointed with the summer athletic program. When it is suggested that badminton become one of the summer sports, Finny revolts. He picks up a ball and tells the group that nothing more is necessary for good sports than a round ball. He then creates a new game which he calls blitzball. The person carrying the ball has everyone else against him. As they begin to play, Finny adds more rules and qualifications until he has worked out a completely new game.

Blitzball becomes the surprise of the summer. Everyone plays it and the success of the game testifies further to Finny's amazing abilities. Gene is glad to have such a person as his roommate.

"Everyone has a moment in history" and that time for Gene is the early months of the war. For him, life will always be influenced by the situation existing in 1942, especially as it affects the carefree lives of the students at Devon school. It is also the summer that he and Phineas walk into the gym and notice the school record for swimming has not been broken. Immediately, Finny jumps into the water and while Gene times him, he breaks the record by .7 of a second. Gene wants him to do it again when there is an official timekeeper present, but Finny says he doesn't care to repeat the performance. In fact, he asks Gene never to mention it. "It's just between you and me," Finny says. Gene cannot understand how someone can break a record and not care about it. He thinks that Finny is too good to be true. That this feat should be kept a secret seems too amazing and it makes "Finny seem too unusual for...rivalry."

As they walk back to the dormitory, Finny suggests that they go to the beach. This is forbidden and also involves a long three-hour bicycle ride which Gene hates. But he agrees to go, and all the way there, Finny sings and tells stories to keep Gene amused. They swim, walk on the beach, eat a hotdog, lie about their ages and get beer, and finally go back to the beach to sleep. There, on the beach, Finny expresses his gratitude for Gene's friendship so sincerely that Gene is almost frightened. "Exposing a sincere emotion nakedly...was the next thing to suicide." Gene almost tells Finny that he is his best friend also, but something holds him back and he says nothing.

Commentary

In the first paragraph, we see that Gene has thought more about the episode of the tree. At the end of the preceding chapter, he concluded that Finny had saved his life. Now he reverses himself and thinks that he was only in the tree because of Finny's influence. Thus, this chapter is the beginning of Gene's self-analysis and recognition of the influence that Finny has on him.

In spite of this insight, however, Gene continues to jump every night, though he hates it. He must jump or else he would lose "face with Phineas and that would have been unthinkable." So Gene is attempting to remain loyal to Finny and trying to fulfill Finny's demand, even though Gene knows that he is "acting against every instinct of his nature." It may be assumed that Gene's fear of the jump and the resentment over having to keep face with Phineas contribute to the motivation for Gene's eventual betrayal of Finny.

Gene, however, is beginning to understand Finny better. He sees that "Finny's life was ruled by inspiration and anarchy" and that Finny prizes his own set of rules. Consequently, the destructive Super Suicide

Society has to meet *every* night. Gene recognizes other qualities in Finny, such as the fact that Finny's mind was "such an opposite from" his.

At this point, Finny's paradoxical nature still prevents the ordered Gene from coming to a full understanding of Finny. For example, Finny says one should speak honestly and truthfully when telling how tall one is. Yet he says to pray because "it might turn out that there is a God." These statements are paradoxical, since one involves complete and absolute honesty, while the other involves insincerity and deception.

We see also in this chapter the extent to which sports are important to Finny. Besides the beauty of the game, they also represent a challenge. This challenge can be seen by the limits that are imposed by the human body, but Finny is the type who revolts against authority, even that dictated by one's own body; consequently, he will attempt any event requiring a little more strength than is usually demanded by the body. Yet, Finny feels that one always wins at sports, forgetting that if one person wins, another must lose. This again is Finny's paradoxical nature carried over into the realm of sports.

Finny's invention of the game of blitzball indicates further his concept of the relationship between life and sports. He has rejected badminton because it was required by the authorities, because it was rather decadent, and because it did not demand any exceptional physical endeavor. In its place he creates the game of blitzball. The name suggests something of the German attack with planes during the Second World War. We must note that Finny creates the game with the same spontaneity to which he responds to any facet of life. In creating the game, he reduces the concept of sports to its most elemental simplicity, which includes an elemental brutality. All one needs for sports is a round ball, and with this ball he proceeds to make up a new game. As the game progresses, Finny adds rules and qualifications, but these are also made spontaneously. Gene notes that Finny "created reverses and deceptions and acts of sheer mass hypnotism which were so extraordinary that they surprised even him." Consequently, we may say that Finny plays the game in the same way that he plays his life—by "reverses and deceptions and acts of sheer mass hypnotism."

Another athletic feat of Finny's is included in this chapter. Finny breaks the school swimming record without ever practicing. It is done on the spur of the moment and cannot become the official record. Gene, of course, wants to make it official, but Finny is not interested in officials or in regulated authority. The victory becomes something tremendous for Gene, and Finny's refusal to acknowledge it makes him "too unusual for rivalry." But for Finny, the victory is artificial. Note even the description of the indoor swimming pool water as being "artificial." Likewise, the challenge of the record was artificial because it was simply a number posted on the wall and was not a reality itself. Finny rejects the swimming pool feat in the same way he rejected the badminton shuttlecock. He tells Gene that only the ocean provides a real challenge, and it takes something really challenging to satisfy Finny.

Finny's feat in the swimming pool becomes for Gene "as dazzling a reversal as" he could possibly imagine. This episode makes Finny into something more than Gene could cope with. He becomes, "in the darkness" where Gene is "forced to hide it," a type of superhuman person who is too unique even to be a rival. This realization means to Gene that he is living in the shadow of Finny's greatness and Gene possibly fears that he will never find himself until he ceases to identify with Finny. This realization contributes also to Gene's eventual jouncing of Finny off the limb. With Finny wounded, Gene might be able to find his own identity.

The trip to the ocean establishes a deeper difference between the two boys. Finny suggests the trip in a "mediocre tone he uses when he is proposing something really outrageous." This again is part of Finny's paradoxical nature. The mediocre tone used in connection with an outrageous event shows Finny's fluctuating nature. Furthermore, we hear that such a trip "risked expulsion," but Finny likes to undertake anything in which there is a risk involved. In contrast, Gene feels that such a trip "blasted the reasonable amount of order [he] wanted to maintain in [his] life." And, in spite of his desire to stay, Gene assents because he cannot refuse anything to Finny for fear of losing face.

At the ocean, we see that Gene stays in only a short time, but Finny swims for an hour. He becomes immersed with all the force and power of the ocean as though, at last, he has found another force that equals his.

After the evening on the beach is completed, the two boys return to the sand to sleep for the night. There Finny joyously apologizes for having dragged Gene away but explains to Gene: "You can't come to the shore with just anybody and you can't come by yourself, and at this teen-age period in life the proper person is your best pal . . . which is what you are." Since Finny is the spontaneous person, this emotional revelation was easy for him to make. But for Gene, who cannot respond to the moment, it is a "courageous thing to say." In other words, it was simple and natural for Finny to say it, but Gene sees it as courageous. Gene feels that he should say the same thing to Finny, but he is held back because he cannot say the simple and the direct thing.

Finally, we should be aware of the importance of water in this chapter. The chapter opens with thoughts of jumping in the river. The game of blitzball is played by the river. There is the swimming episode in the pool and the trip to the ocean. After each of these espisodes, Gene learns more about his friend Finny. It is a though the water allows Gene to be baptized into some truth or revelation about Finny.

CHAPTER 4

Summary

The next morning, Gene awakens first. He watches the dawn break through the sky and notes that Phineas reminds him of the story of Lazarus as the sun and light slowly fell upon Finny's sleeping body. When Phineas wakes, he thinks his night's sleep was the best he has ever had. He wants to go for a swim, but Gene reminds him that there is an important trigonometry test at ten o'clock and it is a three-hour ride back. They want some breakfast, but Finny has lost their combined seventy-five cents.

They arrive back to Devon just in time for Gene's test, which he flunks. It is the first test he has ever flunked. But he doesn't have time to worry about it because the afternoon is taken up with blitzball and the night is scheduled for the meeting of the Super Suicide Society.

That night he tries to catch up with what was happening in trigonometry. Finny keeps interrupting him and tells him that he studies too hard. He wonders if Gene wants to be the class valedictorian and kids him about this, and secretly Gene decides that he would like the honor because this would make him even with Finny. He asks Phineas if it would be all right if he became the head of the class. Phineas answers that he would kill himself out of jealous envy. Suddenly, Gene realizes that Phineas is telling the truth. All summer, Finny has conspired to keep Gene from making good grades. Blitzball, the Super Suicide Society, and the trip to the beach have all been conspiracies to keep Gene from making an "A" in every course. "It was all cold trickery, it was all calculated, it was all enmity."

Now Gene realizes that Phineas is the best athlete but that he is a bad student. He realizes that he himself is a better-than-average athlete and an exceptional student. To keep them even, Finny has been trying to pull Gene's grades down to his level. After this recognition, Gene begins to study exceptionally hard. For weeks he devotes more time to his books than to the various games and he feels much better.

In August, when there are a series of tests coming up, Finny comes into the room and announces that Leper Lepellier plans to jump from the tree that night. Gene doesn't believe it because Leper is such a coward. Finny wants Gene to come and jump. Gene wants to study and gets upset. Finny can't understand because he has always thought that everything comes naturally to Gene. He didn't know that Gene had to work in order to get good grades. Gene realizes that Finny "had made some kind of parallel between" studying and sports. Since sports came easy for Finny, he didn't understand that studying was necessary for Gene. Phineas tells Gene to stay and study because it is really important, more important than jumping out of trees. Then Gene comprehends that there has never been any rivalry between them. He has been entirely wrong about Finny.

When they reach the tree, Finny suggests that they jump together. As they crawl out on the limb, Gene takes a step toward Finny and jounces the limb. With his balance gone, Finny falls throught the leaves and hits "the bank with a sickening, unnatural thud." Gene then jumps into the river, "every trace of his fear forgotten."

Commentary

Chapter 4 opens with the gray dawn and closes with the gray dusk. The image is of one day, even though there is a greater time lapse. The chapter begins on the beach and ends when Gene jounces the limb, making Finny fall. On the beach, the emphasis is already on death. Phineas is asleep but he "looked more dead than asleep." He even makes Gene think of Lazarus, "brought back to life by the touch of God." Thus these death-images set the tone for the accident at the end of the chapter.

Furthermore, the images of Finny and the images of the beach and the morning blend together to suggest that Finny is always immersed in the natural scenery. It is also ironic that it is Gene who is awake during these early hours.

Gene's ordered existence is again emphasized when Finny awakens because Finny immediately asks Gene what time it was. Finny knew that

Gene "was a walking clock." Gene ironically comments that Finny's awakening is like that of Lazarus because of its intensity. Gene will, later, in this chapter think that *he,* himself, is awakening finally from a long sleep during which his world has been sinisterly changed by the calculations of Finny. Attributing a deadly rivalry to Finny will be one of Gene's major mistakes.

Note that Finny goes back into the chilly, white, powerful ocean and returns to Gene full of energy and talk. The elemental joy of swimming in the largest, deepest water in the world has recharged him. Gene, in contrast, worries over time and his trigonometry test, both of which are vivid contrasts to Finny's nature; he is timeless, and the intricate, mathematically embroidered problems are as foreign to him as was the befeathered shuttlecock. The clock's minute divisions of time and the minute divisions of the world of mathematics into trigonometric equations are still of value to Gene. They are safety zones, carefully marked, for thought and emotions too afraid, as yet, to be challenged by the boundless, tree-leaping and ocean-diving vitality of Finny.

Gene flunks his test. This is proof that the conservative Devon education is reflecting Gene's slowly changing nature, but Gene feels only shame over the change. Schoolwork has been his toe hold on the world; he is as insecure in the position of flunkee as he was when he leaped from the tree. He is experiencing a limbo. As a disciple of Finny, he instinctively feels the degree of health Finny's feats offer, but still he hates and resents this alienation from his past.

Gene stages a scholastic comeback, studies double-time and is, naturally and good-naturedly, joshed about it by Finny. Gene equates winning in sports with winning in scholarship. He imagines Finny trying to sabotage his chances for head position of the class. Desperation and fear motivate Gene. Finny's world of sports, however, is healthy and full of fresh air. The competition is of muscle and marrow, not of mind and minuscule letter-symbols. Finny's sports are tangible; he competes against himself, then against others and can feel the *aliveness* of being human when he finishes. Gene's competiveness is mechanical and, instead of sharpening the awareness of life, leaves him with only the dullness of his pencil lead and an emptiness that has flowed onto papers now folded, labeled, and stacked away to be marked. It is impossible that Finny would desire these honors; it is equally foreign to his nature to envy any of Gene's goals.

Finny hopes to find in his roommate Gene a friend who can respond to his own vision of life. He kids Gene about his studying, but his kidding is harmless. Gene, however, sees a "deliberate" design to wreck his chances of being valedictorian, and this distorted view of Finny will be one of the lows he hits in trying to decipher himself. Once Gene had thought of Finny as "too unusual for rivalry." This though has passed. Gene has flunked a test and out of fear has built a protective wall of hatred toward Finny. This animosity exceeds all previous angers within Gene. It will ignite the sudden impulse to cripple Finny, to cripple a destructive quality, a force he doesn't understand,

Finny, in contrast, has shown Gene how to respond to living sufficiently so that Gene is torn, in this chapter, between hating and admiring Finny. The world of Finny surrounds Gene, yet also surrounding Gene is his imagined rivalry with Finny. He says "...I know of too much hate to be contained in a world [beautiful, intoxicating] like this."

The crucial scene at the tree builds in this way: the night before an important examination, Finny suggests that Gene come to watch Leper jump at long last. Gene sees this as Finny's last-ditch effort to cause him to fail for the school's scholastic honors. He attributes to Finny the motivation of jealousy. And to Finny's "questioning" face he attributes a clever mask, disguising envy unprecedented.

Finny's honesty, however, conquers Gene and sends him into a total reversal of feelings. He realizes, once again, Finny's uniqueness precludes jealousy and that a core of unexplainable, irrational anger has menaced his and Finny's friendship and his own self-understanding.

Up in the tree, he reacts as a scared animal might before something he doesn't understand. Gene strikes back, but gently. In an unexplainable, seemingly irreconcilable way, Finny has changed Gene's moderate habits of behavior, his moderate ideas, and his moderate temperament—the latter he has sent spiraling to a high ecstasy and, most recently, to a new, corrupted low of seething hatred. Finny seems to be a friend. He seems also to be, somehow, an enemy.

Like a savage, Gene sees Finny vanish into space. He has banished him with only a slight pressure of the foot, jostling a fragile branch. It happens too quickly to be wholly deliberate; it is animal-like. And feeling free, Gene leaps into the river to cleanse himself.

CHAPTER 5

Summary

No one is allowed at the infirmary for several days. Rumors have it that Finny's leg has been "shattered." Even the masters take it hard that this happened to "one of the few young men who could be free and happy in the summer of 1942."

Throughout these days, Gene wonders how he can defend himself against any charge. Then he realizes that Phineas has told them nothing. One evening, he decides to put on Phineas' clothes. When he is completely clad in Finny's clothes, he feels that he is now Phineas and will "never stumble through the confusion of" his "own character again." That night he even sleeps easier until he wakes up and is confronted with what he has done to Finny.

In the morning, Dr. Stanpole calls Gene over to announce that Phineas is better, but that he will never be able to participate in sports again. In fact, he will be very fortunate to be able to walk again. He asks Gene to help Finny accept the fact that sports are finished for him and sends Gene to see the patient. Gene hears that Finny has asked specifically for him and then Gene understands that "Phineas would say nothing behind" his back. The accusation will be face to face.

When Gene sees Finny, he is aware first of all of a tremendous change. Phineas looks smaller than before and not so healthy. Gene immediately asks Finny what happened in the tree. Finny can't explain it except to say he just fell. He tells how he turned to reach out for Gene's hand and he remembers how Gene's face had an "awfully funny expression." Gene asks him again if he knows what made him fall. Finny does admit that he had a funny feeling but has dismissed it from his mind. He even apologizes for the feeling.

When Gene hears this "sincere drugged apology for having suspected the truth," he realizes that Finny would always tell the truth. Consequently, Gene decides to confess to Finny, but Dr. Stanpole comes in and sends him away. Soon after, Finny is sent to Boston in an ambulance.

The summer ends in an atmosphere of unreality, and Gene goes home for a month's vacation. Returning to school, he drops by Finny's home and finds him "propped by white hospital-looking pillows." Finny is very pleased by the visit and wants to know if Gene has brought him something from down South. They talk for a while of insignificant things while Gene wonders how he is going to tell Finny the truth. After more thought, he confesses that he had "deliberately jounced the limb so" Finny would fall off. Phineas immediately denies it and tells Gene to sit down. When

Gene continues, Finny threatens to hit him. Finny still refuses to believe Gene and tells him to go away. Suddenly, Gene realizes that he is injuring Finny again and that it is worse for Finny to know the truth. He wants only to make it all up to him, but he has to do it at school, not here in Finny's house.

He tells Phineas that he has to leave because he is already a day late. Finny tells Gene not to start living by the rules, and Gene says he won't, even though he knows that that is "the biggest lie of all."

Commentary

The conflict of the Second World War re-enters when the masters see Finny's injury in terms of striking down "one of the few young men who could be free and happy in the summer of 1942." But this war does not enter into Gene's mind. He is more concerned with his own personal fears. Now they involve whether or not Finny will accuse him of the accident. He thinks at first that Finny is too sick to accuse him and then comes to the realization that Finny is not the type of person to accuse a friend behind his back. Instead, Finny will make the accusation directly. This reasoning on Gene's part is his attempt to understand Finny and himself. We must note that Gene is totally wrong in his evaluation of Finny because Phineas never makes any type of accusation against Gene.

One evening before Gene is allowed to see Finny, he decides to dress in his friend's clothes. Here he is trying again to become Finny or become a part of Finny's world. He thinks: "I was Phineas, Phineas to the life," and he believes that he will never "stumble through the confusions of my own character again." We now understand that Gene's aim is to become as much like Finny as possible and that he can only do so by having destroyed a part of Finny's nature, that is, by crippling him. Ironically, however, Gene will begin to discover his own nature now that Finny is wounded and will continue for a long time to "stumble through the confusions" of his own character.

When the doctor announces that "sports are finished" for Finny, Gene feels as though the doctor is pronouncing Finny to be dead or at least drastically changed. Later we discover that Gene rejects sports also as though the comment had been applied to him.

In his interview with Finny, Gene arrives looking more like the patient than the visitor. He is still living in his fear that Finny will accuse him. Consequently, there seems to be the ironic reversal of patient looking cheerful and visitor looking sickly. In one sense, Gene's and Finny's roles in relation to each other will be somewhat reversed. Gene's remarks are described as being "instinctive like the reactions of someone cornered." Previous to this, Gene has never acted instinctively but Finny has always done so. Consequently, when Finny tells that he turned in the tree to "get hold off" Gene, Gene's first reaction is to flinch violently away from Finny and to ask: "To drag me down too." In terms of the way that Gene has been thinking about Finny, he thinks that his friend was out to destroy him in the same way that Gene attempted to destroy Finny. Thus, we have the simple, but ironic, parallel with the earlier scene where Finny had reached out and saved Gene from falling out of the tree.

Gene's desire to become a part of Finny is again suggested when he tells Finny that the accident affects him as though it had happened to him personally. Gene is still trying to become a part of Phineas. Consequently, in talking with Finny, Gene wonders what Finny would do if their roles could be reversed. He sees that Finny is ashamed of himself for "having suspected the truth." He knows that Finny would always tell the truth and he decides to confess to Finny. But we must be aware that his decision to confess is a result of his attempt to do what Finny would do. In other words, in trying to confess, he is still trying to imitate Finny. It will be some time yet before he will act out of his own character. He is, however, prevented from telling by arrival of Dr. Stanpole.

The summer session ended in "an atmosphere of reverie and unreality." It was not real for Gene because he was deprived of Finny and had not yet developed any values of his own. He had to resort to the type of living which preceded his acquaintance with Finny. Thus, after his month's vacation, he feels the need now of making the confession to Finny. But this time the confession is not made in an attempt to emulate Finny's actions. For the first time, Gene is beginning to develop a sense of his own values. He is developing personal integrity which necessitates this confession, and so he is arriving at a growing maturity.

The images here suggest that Gene is, basically, a savage individual. He feels like "a wild man who had stumbled in from the jungle to tear the place apart." Later, even Leper will refer to Gene as having a concealed "savage nature." It was this repressed savageness (or blind impulse as it is later called) which motivated Gene to jounce the limb. When he confesses, and when Finny refuses to believe him, Gene wants Finny to hit him or kill him because that was how he felt when he jounced the limb. In other words, Gene recognizes now in himself some of his savage nature which has no place in the world of civilized society.

After the scene is ended, Finny tells Gene not to start living by the rules back at Devon. Gene agrees not to, but "that was the most false thing, the biggest lie of all." Without the presence of Finny, Gene feels that he will definitely revert back to his life of conformity and adherence to rules. It was this violation of rules earlier with Finny which brought forward his savage qualities. That is, as long as Gene had been able to live his life by obeying certain established rules and as long as he was able to conform to the rules of society, he functioned well. But with Finny, he acts as a free man — but as Finny's man — unhampered by the dictates of society. This excess freedom proved to be too much for Gene and he grew into the savage man who tried to destroy out of blind impulse. Once more, back into the realm of conformity, Gene will be able to constrain himself.

CHAPTER 6

Summary

The fall was different at Devon. The masters try to stress continuity but Gene knows that everything is false. The summer session had been so free and easy that a reassumption of rules and routine seems immature. Gene has the same room he had shared with Finny, but he is now alone.

Students like Brinker Hadley (who is one of the class leaders) seem out of place because they weren't there during the summer session. Gene finds himself being late for appointments — something that has never before happened to him. Today, he was to report to the crew house, where he was to assume the duties of assistant crew manager — a position which was reserved for the crippled and maimed. The crew house is on the lower river — the Naguamsett. This river runs behind the school and is never used because it is dirty and ugly.

The crew manager, Quackenbush, is annoyed at Gene for being late. He begins to pick on Gene and orders him around. Since no senior and no healthy person ever held this position, Quackenbush assumes that something is wrong, but Gene knows that Quackenbush's "flat black eyes would never detect" the trouble. He also realizes that Quackenbush has never been liked and furthermore was not a part of the "gypsy summer." The two get into an argument over trivial matters and when Quackenbush calls Gene a "maimed son-of-a-bitch," they get into a fight that ends when they fall into the dirty waters of the lower river.

Gene leaves feeling as though he has fought the first battle for Finny. While returning to the dormitory, he meets Mr. Ludsbury, one of the regular masters. The teacher questions Gene about his wet clothes and then reprimands him for failing to observe rules during the summer session. Before leaving, he tells Gene there is a long-distance call waiting for him.

The call is from Phineas, who wants to wish him luck on his first day of school and wants to know if Gene is saving his place as roommate. Finny mentions that Gene must have been crazy when he dropped by for a visit. Finny even apologizes for thinking funny things about Gene. Then he wants to know what sports Gene is going out for. When he hears about the job as assistant crew manager, Finny is dumbfounded. Gene tries to explain that he is too busy for sports. It is as though when Dr. Stanpole said, "Sports are finished," the doctor had been speaking to both him and Finny. Phineas says that Gene *has* to play sports now for him. Then Gene realizes that this must have been his purpose in pushing Finny off the limb, that is, "to become a part of Phineas."

Commentary

In Chapter 6, we see Gene acting without Finny's being present. Now Gene can perhaps come to more realizations about himself. First of all, he sees that after the summer session it is impossible to return to all the traditions and continuity stressed by the school. He feels that the past three months have completely changed his approach to life. During the summer, they had been undirected. Now the class leaders who are beginning to take over seem out of place in the light of the past three months.

Other changes are indicated in this chapter. We hear that Gene is now often late for appointments. We also hear that there are two rivers at Devon. The second river is in complete contrast to the Devon River. The Devon is clean and fresh, but the second river, the Naguamsett, is "ugly, saline, fringed with marsh, mud and seaweed." While Finny was there they were seen only in terms of the Devon. Now Gene is alone and he goes to take up a job at the lower, or dirty, river.

On the way to the river, Gene thinks about Finny as he was in the past. He remembers a time when Finny was riding down the river with one foot on the "prow of a canoe like a river god," and how with a "veering of the canoe," Finny "would tumble into the water." These recollections emphasize Finny as the "demigod," the person who transcends rivalry and also suggests the water motif, except here Finny falls into the water rather than being pushed.

Gene's new position — assistant crew manager — is a job that Finny would spurn. The job requires little or no work and is "usually taken by boys with some physical disability." We then wonder if Gene is accepting the type of job that Finny would have had to accept, now that he is crippled. In other words, Gene has a job which Finny would have to accept because of Gene's crippling Finny. Consequently, when Gene and Quackenbush get into an argument, Gene, for the first time, does not back away. He is told by Quackenbush to "go to hell," but Gene has been in hell ever since the accident. He resents Quackenbush because of the loss he "was fighting to endure," and thus, when Quackenbush calls him a "maimed son-of-a-bitch," Gene strikes out at him. Gene now has added insight to see into his nature as he realizes that it is almost as though he is maimed, and he knows that he is now fighting a battle for Finny instead of against him.

As they fight, they fall into the ugly, dirty saline waters of the Naguamsett and, unlike the jumps into the Devon River where he emerged clean and fresh, he comes out of this lower river feeling dirty and in need of a bath. But this allows him to see that he fought the battle only partly for Phineas and partly for himself. He knows now that there is a partial identification with Finny, but he is at least coming to some sense of his own self.

Going back to the dormitory, Gene meets Mr. Ludsbury, one of the regular masters. He is strongly reprimanded for his behavior and Gene "said nothing..." We get the impression that if Finny had been there, he could have countered the criticism with some fantastic story, but Gene merely concurs with the criticism and accepts it.

Gene goes to Mr. Ludsbury's study in order to return a long-distance call he has recieved. The call is from Phineas, wondering if Gene is still as crazy as he sounded when he made the confession. We see that Phineas does not believe Gene's confession because he is all "friendliness, simply outgoing affection" which cannot conceive of a dubious or treacherous action. In fact, Finny is much concerned as to whether Gene is saving a place for him as roommate. Finny is, however, more concerned over what sports Gene is going out for. Gene feels that when Dr. Stanpole said, "Sports are finished," he was speaking for both Finny and Gene, yet Finny's values are built basically on sports. Finny tells Gene: "Listen, if I can't play sports *you're* going to play them for me." Then Gene realizes that he has always wanted to be a part of Phineas. He thinks that, perhaps, his secret purpose in jouncing the limb was "to become a part of Phineas." Consequently, in wounding Phineas, Gene has brought Finny down to his level or below it, so that Finny will now be partially dependent upon Gene and, in this way, Gene can become an integral part of Finny's life.

CHAPTER 7

Summary

Gene has "to shower and to wash off the sticky salt of the Naguamsett river." The Devon River was clean, but he had never before been into the lower river. Brinker Hadley comes in later and congratulates Gene on having the room to himself. He jokingly suggests that Gene chose Finny knowing that Finny wouldn't be back. He even suggests that Gene fixed it. Gene feels too uncomfortable with this type of talk and suggests a smoke in the "Butt Room," which is the basement of the dormitory. When they enter the room, Brinker jokingly turns Gene over for the "rankest treachery," that is, "doing away with his roommate so he could have a whole room to himself." Gene thinks that they are carrying the joke too far, but immediately the others take up the charge and accuse Gene of killing his roommate. Gene realizes that he must play along or else. He constructs a fabulous story of theft, blackmail, love, and then comes to the part involving Finny's accident, but he is unable to speak the final words—"pushed him out of the tree." After recovering his confidence, he announces that he has to study. While leaving he hears a voice say, "he came all the way down here and didn't even have a smoke."

The fall days pass slowly. The members of the class help gather the local apple crop, since the harvesters are off to the war. Some heavy snows fall earlier than usual and two hundred people are needed to help clear a railroad yard nearby. Going to the train, Gene meets Leper, who is out sketching birds. Gene discovers that Leper is just touring around on skis looking for a beaver dam. He leaves Leper and heads for the station.

The snow-shoveling soon becomes a tedious and monotonous job. They work slowly and quietly until late afternoon, when there is then enough cleared to allow the first train through. It is a troop train filled with young inductees. They look as though they are going places while the students "seemed to be nothing but children playing among heroic men."

Coming back, the students talk of how long the war might last. Quackenbush thinks he will stay at Devon through the entire year and then enlist. Walking back to the school, they run into the lone figure of Lepellier. He tells them that he found the beaver dam in one of the tributaries to the Devon. Gene intercedes before some of the students tell Leper how stupid he is to be looking for beavers when there is a war going on. But Brinker is so agitated he maintains he will enlist the next day.

This thought breaks upon Gene's consciousness. "To slam the door impulsively on the past" is what he has spent his summer trying to do. After more thought, Gene decides that he will enlist immediately. When he bounds up the stairs to his room, he notices that the lights are on. Finny is sitting in Gene's chair and "everything that had happened throughout the day faded."

Commentary

The "baptism" Gene refers to occurs after he fights with Quackenbush and falls into the Naguamsett River. The Naguamsett has been described as being ugly, muddy and slough-like; therefore, within the loose biblical allegory we have discovered (concerning Evil's invasion of an Edenic setting, the nature and the source of Evil) that the fall into the slough can be interpreted as a kind of reverse baptism, which will color many of Gene's upcoming actions. One of Gene's sins was attributing a perverseness to Finny's persuasive personality, and after Gene attempted to destroy Finny, he must now face daily the realization that the only evil was within himself, and was a manufactured, defensive mechanism. Growing into manhood, Gene discovers, will involve an objective appraisal of one's emotions, their sources, and an honest "Know Thyself" appraisal of one's developing values. Because the biblical allegory is loose, the structure of the book can be deepened by also seeing Gene's growth as an epic, or Greek-like, odyssey of youth sailing for the adult homeland. Considering the book in these terms, note the importance of water to the young odyssey sailor and how often the initiation-toward-maturity scenes involve either oceans, or the two rivers (the Beautiful and the Ugly), rain pools, and even (a form of water) snow, how he sometimes succumbs to inertia (as did Odysseus) before finally ridding his land (himself, in Gene's case) of destroyers (immature, fearful reactions and hypocrisy for Gene).

Gene washes himself after the fight in which he has been jeered at by Quackenbush. Quackenbush, significantly, used catcalls which describe Finny, words like "maimed." This has served to tear any rationalizing or forgetful scab from Gene's guilt. It lies open now and Gene's falling into the salty river intensifies his evaluation of the relationship between Finny and himself. Showering, however, eases the raw smart of guilt, for the present.

Brinker Hadley's playful accusation of Gene is painfully embarrassing. The dramatic irony of our knowing the truth is extended from this isolated episode involving two boys to a mock-trial scene in the basement Butt Room. This parody will be paralleled, not in a basement, but in the upper story of the assembly room, and instead of being mock, will be climactically violent.

The reader should note the irony of, besides the situation, such statements as, "In our free democracy...the truth will out," and "To the dungeon with you." Democracy has an added dimension: its connotations are of brotherhood and loyalty, the qualities which Gene has violated. Brinker's "Here's your prisoner..."is a joke, but Gene's knowledge of his guilt, again ironically, makes him his *own* prisoner. Because Finny has refused to believe Gene's confession the weight of Gene's act is still as heavy as if he had never confessed. He cannot confess, even jokingly, to end the humiliating mock inquiry. All that Gene can manage is an offhand reference to Brinker's acting like Dr. Watson. The boys then leave off the trial, but Brinker is left the butt of a joke, and Gene has provoked Quackenbush's hatred and now that of Brinker. This is a new role for Gene to see himself in but, in truth, he hates himself as well.

Like seasons, even hate becomes boresome and passes, and emphasis shifts to an interest in the war—at first (as was Gene's first trial) only a mock, playful interest before a later vivid realism. And interest shifts to Leper. Leper is to figure, eventually, as the school's war representative and, at this point, he comes to the foreground as a sketcher of birds and trees. Gene describes him as a scarecrow, wearing odd bits of clothing and relic-like skis, and looking for a beaver dam while the rest are digging out a snowed-in railroad yard. The war's interest, apparently, is passing him by, as is much of Devon's activity.

Gene, meanwhile, helps clear the snowy tracks to allow passage of a troop train, and, watching it, feels that their own worth is as childlike as Leper's own winter ramblings, compared to the waving soldiers packed in the train. His feeling of futility began with seeing Leper as the school's representative, then shifts to an inclusion of all of Devon's boys. The surge of war crests over the school. Brinker announces his upcoming enlistment and Gene also decides to "slam the door impulsively on the past, to shed everything down to my last bit of clothing, break the pattern of my life...." The war is violent and Gene feels a need for a violent counterpart to his action against Finny. Gene realizes the difficulty of defining evil. He says, "...there was always something deadly lurking in anything I loved. ...And if it wasn't there, as for example with Phineas, then I put it there myself."

Thus far, he is aware that evil is often projected from within oneself, but his mistake now is declaring an allegiance to war (under the guise of patriotism) because of its ready-made enemy. In war, there are no tangled knots of motivation to unravel for oneself; there is only the predefined target and the command, and then—without responsibility for one's own—to destroy the enemy.

Then he finds Phineas. Phineas, the essence of vibrant life, now maimed, comes home. A life force confronts Gene just as he has decided on a course of action dedicated to destructive killing.

CHAPTER 8

Summary

Phineas notices Gene's work clothes, and when he hears that Gene has been working on the railroad, Finny is amused at the new mode of life at Devon. He also asks about the rumor that there are no maids. Gene explains that there is a war going on, and Finny wonders, "Is there?"

Gene makes up Finny's bed for him and after further talk, they sleep. Again in the morning, Phineas asks about the lack of maids and at the same time tells Gene to hand him his crutch. Suddenly, Gene realizes that the past summer is going to be succeeded by a winter of snows and crutches.

Brinker Hadley comes in from next door, and on seeing Finny, says that Gene's "little plot didn't work so well after all." Gene feels as though he can't face this joke any longer and changes the subject by talking about enlisting. He explains to Finny that after the railroad work, many of them had talked about enlisting. Phineas seems shocked at the idea and suggests they all go take a shower. Gene suddenly realizes that Phineas needs him and doesn't want him to enlist. Quickly then, the war "passed away" and "peace had come back to Devon for" Gene.

On the first day back, Phineas wants to skip class and wander around the school. He says they can pretend that he fainted and that Gene had to care for him. Even though the gym is at the other side of the campus, and even though the icy walks are treacherous for crutches, Finny heads straight for this favorite building. By the time they reach the gym, Finny is sweating and seems overly pale.

Once inside, Finny says that Gene will have to be "the big star now." He tells Gene to chin himself. Finny can't understand why Gene did not go out for some of the sports and refuses to accept the explanation that sports are not so important when there is a war going on. Phineas refuses to believe in the war. He explains that it is all a trick perpetrated by some fat old men in Washington. Gene tries to disagree, but Finny is adamant in his belief. When Gene wants to know how Finny received his insight while the rest of the people are in the dark, Phineas' face freezes and he answers: "Because I've suffered." After this desperate revelation, silence covers the two boys. Gene breaks it by chinning himself thirty times.

After this, Finny says that he was aiming at the 1944 Olympics but now he will coach Gene instead. Once again Gene mentions the war only to be told to ignore that fantasy. From then on, both get up at six A.M. and train before breakfast. Finny tells Gene what to do, and later in the day Gene returns the favor by helping Finny with his studies. Both seem to improve tremendously and Gene feels that with the exercise he is growing bigger all at once. After some time, Gene begins to wonder if Finny is right about there being no war.

Commentary

Finny's first comment to Gene tries to re-establish the old friendly relationship between them. He laughs at Gene's clothes because they are so different from what he is accustomed to seeing Gene wear. The point is, however, that Finny has lost out on something. A new element has been introduced into Devon in Finny's absence, and Finny senses that he is not a part of it. Therefore he must ridicule this element, this work on the railroad because of the war. Furthermore, due to his crippled leg, Finny could not participate in this type of work anyway and thus refuses to recognize its value.

We begin to see a change in Gene. For the first time, he offers an objective and correct criticism of Finny. Phineas is disgruntled because there are no maids, but Gene accepts that as a part of the war effort. Gene says: "My unselfishness was responding properly to the influences of 1942. In these past months Phineas and I had grown apart on this; I felt certain disapproval of him for grumbling about a lost luxury." In other words, Finny gone, Gene begins to develop a sense of values independent of those advocated by Finny. He is beginning to become an individual, but with Finny's return, he will once again become a part of Finny's world.

Furthermore, prior to Finny's return Gene had "welcomed each new day as though it were a new life, where all past failures and problems were erased," but now with Finny back in school, he must return to his earlier life with all his earlier problems. The images throughout this section emphasize the contrast between the past summer of carefree actions and the present winter "of snow and crutches." Gene will now have to become a crutch for Finny.

That Finny needs Gene now is brought out in the next scene. Brinker comes into the room and renews his painful joke about Gene's plot to do away with a roommate. This joke is too bitter for Gene and he changes the subject as soon as possible to that of enlisting in the armed service. Phineas is visibly shocked at the idea, and Gene realizes that Finny needs him. He also recognizes that he is "the least trustworthy person" Finny has ever known, but is still glad that Finny needs him. Almost immediately the war fades away and Gene assumes his place as an aid to Finny, and then Gene feels that "peace had come back to Devon for me."

The reader should again be aware of the water imagery surrounding this revelation. When the subject of enlistment came up, Phineas immediately suggests a shower. Then Gene recognizes that the "war swept over like a wave at the seashore" and he was left "treading water as before.

As Finny and Gene walk about the campus, Gene is aware of a difference in Finny. There is now the danger provided by the icy walks and the "smooth, slick marble, more treacherous even than the icy walks." This last reference provides us with a foreshadowing of Finny's fall down the marble stairs later on.

On this first day back, Finny suggests that they skip class so that he can see parts of the campus. For the first time, Gene openly criticizes and contradicts Finny by telling him, "You're no one to cut classes." But Gene does acquiesce and goes with Finny toward the gym, It was a long walk and by the time they arrive, Finny is exhausted. "The leg in its cast was like a sea anchor dragged behind." (note again the water and sea imagery). The fact that Finny is so exhausted reminds both Gene and the reader that he is far from being well.

When they arrive at the gym, Gene feels here that he has completely escaped the war and is surrounded by the secure world of sports. A conflict arises between the two friends as Gene tries to explain that sports aren't important now that there is a war going on. To Finny, sports have always been important, and since he can't participate in the war, he refuses to believe in it. He tells Gene about his theory that the war is a big joke being perpetrated by old men in Washington. But Finny, the cripple, does not control Gene now so completely; Gene has begun to live his own life and refuses to accept Finny's extraordinary explanation of the war. He forces the issue to a crisis by asking why Finny should get the joke and no one else. Finny's response destroys all of Gene's chances of becoming a separate individual. He answers that he sees the truth because *he has suffered*. This answer destroys Gene's chances of opposing Finny because Gene knows that Finny's suffering is a result of the accident in the tree. Gene's guilt forces him now to become again subservient to Finny's character. This is represented by Gene's immediately going to the bar and chinning himself thirty times, a feat which is in imitation of something Finny would do.

After this crucial and brutal revelation, Finny must disclose further depths of his wishes. He had wanted to train for the 1944 Olympics and now must instead coach Gene. Again Gene tries to mention the war and told to forget that fantasy. Gene soon realizes that it is only through a "continuous use of the imagination" that he could "hold out against Finny's moving offensive in favor of peace." We know later that Finny refuses to recognize the war because he has been unable to enlist and if he can't take a part in anything, he refuses to recognize the importance of that thing.

Gene's chief problem becomes his attempts to maintain his own view of the war against Finny's fantasy. In one paragraph, Gene says three times that "Of course I didn't believe him." But nevertheless he senses that he is slowly accepting Finny's view, even though he rationally knows that it is absurd.

During the ensuing weeks, Gene spends much of his time tutoring Finny in studies and being tutored by Finny in sports. The image here is significant. Finny leans up against a *tree* and watches while Gene practices his running in great circles around the tree. Slowly as Gene develops greater athletic powers, he sees that Finny is, after all, not so great. After this particular feat, he returns to Finny and notes that Finny "seemed smaller too. Or perhaps it was only that I, inside the same body, had felt myself all at once grown bigger." Thus, Gene is balancing on a precarious fence. He is on the verge of accepting again Finny's views and at the end of the chapter he temporarily falls into this trap, and on the other hand, he is beginning to see Finny in the correct perspective – that he is not so godlike, but simply another human being.

CHAPTER 9

Summary

Gene finds it easy to lapse into Finny's world of peace. He is not even disturbed that Leper became the first from Devon to enlist. In fact, it makes the war seem more unreal, since Leper has never been concerned with anything except his snails.

A recruiter from the ski troops comes to Devon and shows pictures of the ski troops in action. Leper quietly announces that he is going to enlist, and a week later, he is gone. "For a few days the war was more unimaginable than ever." One day, Brinker finds a way to account for the enigma. After every big campaign or accomplishment, everyone says that it was Leper who was leading the endeavor. During all the talk about Leper, Phineas never says a word; in fact, he even slowly draws Gene away from the regular crowd who do talk about Leper's feats.

One Saturday afternoon, Phineas announces that they should organize a "Winter Carnival." There has never been one before, but Finny begins to plan one. He is even going to assign Leper the job of beautifying the place until Gene reminds him that Leper is gone. Gene gets others to join in with the idea because it is the first thing Finny has attempted since he came back to Devon.

The Saturday scheduled for the games arrives. Phineas has bought the prizes for the winners of the various games to be played. There are statues of all the teachers made of soft snow, and there is an improvised ski jump. Brinker has been able to get some hard cider, which he guards carefully.

As soon as all are gathered, Brinker yells for someone to start the games. He is so insistent that Finny announces that Brinker is next. The sound of a bullfight is played on the bugle and then all the boys attack Brinker and take his cider away from him. After the ruckus, Finny calls for some fire in order to officially declare the games open.

When the day is about over, Finny announces that Gene Forrester is "our Olympic candidate" and will now qualify for the decathlon. Gene knows that he can do almost anything Finny wants him to. He realizes that "it wasn't the cider which made me surpass myself, it was this liberation we had torn from the gray encroachments of 1943, the escape we had concocted, this afternoon of momentary, illusory special and separate peace."

At this point a telegram arrives for Gene, and Finny takes it, thinking it is from the Olympic Committee. After glancing at it, he hands it to Gene. It is from Leper pleading for help, asking Gene to come to him at once.

Commentary

A film shown at the school depicts angel-like soldier-skiers on virgin white slopes and these heavenly trappings of war heighten Gene's disbelief in an actual national struggle. Leper, however, is converted by the film to actually enlisting. Thus, during this chapter, for Gene, the world of war becomes alternately nonexistent (Finny's vision) or unreal and unlikely (since Leper's enlistment).

Leper has left, however, saying that war is a test of survival, depending on one's evolvements. Gene's imagination is caught by Leper's question, because gradually he has realized his own evolving nature, triggered to change by Finny, and he is anxious about "the still hidden parts" of himself.

Gene, aware that he is not yet able to resist completely the imaginative, exciting vision of life Finny exudes, lapses once more into a separate peace of his and Finny's. And it is then that Finny sparks the class members into organizing a "traditional" winter carnival, in much the same way that he organized the Super Suicide Society and the game of blitzball. He does this to draw attention, once more, away from the war, to his world — the world of sports. In contrast to the depressing winter countryside, Finny's plans are colored with the preposterous: winter carnivals are probably against the school's rules, ski jumps are planned on flat ground, and forbidden hard cider is to be cooled in snow banks for the victors of the carnival.

Note that the book's descriptive sections have changed as a background for the action. Finny's conception is of a carnival, yet the mood outside is of an incongruous color. The weather is stone gray, the war exists for everyone but him and Gene as dimensional background, and, most important, the carnival will be held next to the Naguamsett. Finny has been crippled and Gene is often limping psychologically in step with him. The peace of Gene's ordered life before Finny, and Finny's loss of flowing athleticism after Gene, cannot exist any longer beside the still, calm, and green Devon River. The Naguamsett with all of its imperfections must be, logically, now the setting for the boys and their carnival.

The carnival, conceived to revere sports, begins with a "barbaric" trumpet blast, and the boys battle in mock war for the cider and after relieving latent violence they urge Finny to begin the games. He seizes the *Iliad,* the Greek epic celebrating the Trojan War, and lights it (symbolically attempting to eradicate war) as a sacred fire.

The games are exuberant, intoxicating, and unrestrained. Gene imagines himself, on the low ski jump, to actually be soaring in flight, "hurtling high and far through space." He has caught the fever again of Finny's "magic gift for existing primarily in space." Gene sees himself being awarded the wreath for best athlete (the prize which Finny would have been awarded if he were not maimed), and begins his qualifying feats by walking the half-circle of statues on his hands and following that by balancing on his head on an icebox on top of the prize table. These feats of Gene's are, significantly, upside down; they have no relation to the exacting reality he has been laboring for. He is still a portion of Finny; he is excelling in Finny's space-world; he is as yet unable to stand on his own two feet.

Propitiously, a telegram is delivered amidst Gene's reversal. Leper has escaped from the war. At last, the shock of a real war, and human desperation resulting from that war, occurs within Finny and within Gene as they read the telegram.

Gene says he faced the telegram in advance, sensing destruction; he says further, "That was what I learned to do that winter." Thus, once again, he has been wrenched violently from Finny's world of pulsating gypsy moods into the encroachments of 1943. The "separate peace," the world inhabited by just Finny and Gene, has once more been severed.

CHAPTER 10

Summary

The journey from school to Leper's house was only the first of many monotonous and routine trips that Gene takes during the closing years of the war. He travels all night and reaches Leper's house in the early morning. He has been thinking all night about what Leper meant when he wired that he "escaped" from the army.

When he arrives at Leper's house, Leper meets him at the door and leads him into the dining room, explaining that he stays in this room all the time because one can always count on three meals a day appearing in there. Gene tries to make some jokes with Leper, but soon notices that Leper is disturbed and nervous. Gene then tries to be serious and asks Leper how long he will be home. Again Leper explains that he has escaped. Then he becomes agitated and accuses Gene of thinking of him as not normal. He wonders if Gene thinks of him as being a "psycho." This strange word opens up new worlds to Gene. It sounds so harsh and ugly.

Gene tells Leper that these new army words are disgusting and Leper responds that Gene will soon be trapped. This annoys Gene and he tells Leper to "stick to your snails." Leper then accuses Gene of being "a savage underneath"; to prove his point, Leper reminds Gene of the time he "knocked Finny out of the tree." Suddenly Gene becomes infuriated and calls Leper a "crazy bastard." By now Leper is laughing and reminds Gene that he crippled Finny for life. Gene knocks Leper's chair over, and Leper lies on the floor laughing and crying. Mrs. Lepellier comes in and stops the fracas. She explains that Leper is ill. Gene wants to leave, but Leper wants him to stay for lunch. Gene is so ashamed that he accepts the invitation to stay for lunch.

Afterward, Mrs. Lepellier suggests the boys take a walk. Outside Gene mentions Brinker and suddenly Leper sees an image of "Snow White with Brinker's face on her." He begins to sob and seems unable to stop.

When he is finally able to regain his composure, he explains that in the service he always saw different faces on different bodies. He tells Gene many more stories, that a man came in carrying an amputated leg, and that a corporal changed into a woman, and other strange and bizarre incidents. Suddenly Gene cannot stand it any longer and cries out: "This has nothing to do with me! Nothing at all! I don't care!" He then turns and runs away from Leper, leaving him still "telling his story into the wind." Gene feels he has heard too much and feels it has nothing to do with him.

Commentary

The adolescent games played by the boys in the last chapter fade rapidly from sight as soon as Gene receives the telegram. The innocence of youth is interrupted by the reality of the war from which Leper thinks he has escaped. In actuality, the games invented by Finny for the winter carnival were an attempt to escape from the greater war. And even though Leper had written that he had escaped, we soon realize that man can escape from nothing. Consequently, by the end of the chapter, we will understand that Gene's attempt to escape the war through his attachment to Finny is just as "psycho" as is Leper's escaping from it. Both involve dangerous attitudes.

Gene must, however, take the trip. We have seen him too long in the presence of Finny, and now this trip suggests an act which separates Gene from Phineas. Gene must now act on his own and must see himself as someone other than Finny sees him.

At Leper's house, Gene thinks that Leper's acts are selfish, but he fails to realize that his own acts have been also selfish. In some ways, everything that Leper has done is reflected in Gene's past and present behavior. For example, Leper wonders if Gene thinks him normal. This question immediately returns us to Gene's jouncing of the limb and we must ponder the normality of this act. The word "psycho" enters the conversation and suddenly Gene is seized with fear because he realizes what an intense conflict can make a person do; that is, his own intense conflict with Phineas caused Gene to jounce the limb.

Throughout the scene, Leper uses words and unpleasant descriptions, and narrates stories about his conflicts until Gene feels that he is being drawn into something ugly. Gene does not want to be brought into the war this way. He likes the quiet peace of Devon, and Leper's narration makes him look at the adult world. As he tries to quiet Leper, Leper turns on him and tells Gene how much a savage Gene has always been underneath. He reminds Gene of "that time you knocked Finny out of the tree...that time you crippled him for life." At this point, Gene's savage nature does once again emerge as he knocks Leper out of his chair. Thus, in the same way that he made Finny fall from the tree, he forces Leper to fall from the chair. Both acts are part of Gene's savage nature or his blind impulse which he has not yet learned to control, since he refuses at this point to function in the adult world.

As Gene thinks over his behavior, he feels that Leper might be essentially right about him. He does have a savage nature underneath all the exterior pose. As they walk together through the quiet, peaceful, New England winter landscape, Gene sees that his nature is primitive. Consequently, Leper's narration of his terrible experiences becomes too much for Gene to bear. As the crust of snow beneath them begins to crack, so does Gene begin to crack. He screams to Leper: "I don't give a damn! Do you understand that? This has nothing to do with me! Nothing at all! I don't care!" In other words, Gene is trying to escape the real world and return to the wonderful winter games created by Finny. He cannot yet face the real adult world of confusion and guilt because he has not yet solved his private war which is still being fought on Devon campus.

CHAPTER 11

Summary

Gene wanted only to see Phineas because with him "there was not conflict except between athletes." He finds him in the middle of a snowball fight and he yells to Gene that they need him on their side. No one bothers to ask about Leper until much later and then only in a casual manner. The snowball fight continues with various people changing sides until everyone ultimately turns on Finny. After it is over, Phineas comments that it was a fine fight.

Later Gene asks Finny if he "ought to get into fights like that." Phineas believes that his leg is getting much stronger. That night, Brinker comes into the room and questions Gene about Leper. He drives so relentlessly to the truth that Gene has to admit that Leper is "out of his mind." Brinker is disturbed because it reflects on the class. He adds that now they have two men "sidelined for the Duration." In answer to Gene's query, Brinker indicates that Finny is the other and even Phineas has to agree. Then suddenly, all of Finny's special inventions fade away and they are back into reality.

More and more enlistment officers appear on the campus. One day, Brinker tells Gene that he is putting off enlisting simply because he pities

Finny. He suggests that it would be better for Gene if everything was
cleared up about Finny's accident. He leaves Gene confused as to the
implications of these comments. Gene then devotes himself to helping
Phineas with his Latin. The Latin text involves war, and Finny doesn't
want to believe in a war which occurred some two thousand years ago, but
he must believe in something; so he tells Gene that he believes in him. At
first, Finny reveals, he did not believe the story about Leper, but then, this
morning at chapel, he saw Leper hiding in the shrubbery next to the chapel.
If war can make Leper into a psycho, then war must be real.

At 10:05 P.M. Brinker and three cohorts come into the room and take
Gene and Finny to the First Building. Even though they are curious, they
are told to wait and see what is going to happen. They are led to the huge
assembly room — a room whose atmosphere is so somber that all practical
jokes are out of the question. Brinker asks a prayer and then tells Phineas
to tell the story of his fall in his own words. It is revealed that the group
is investigating Phineas' accident because the war needs every able-bodied
man. Brinker explains that they do not want any rumors and suspicions
left unanswered.

Phineas maintains that there is nothing to tell. He simply fell out of
the tree because he lost his balance. He has, however, had the "feeling
that the tree did it by itself." Phineas is asked if anyone else was in the
tree with him. Finny explains that he can't remember all the details. Someone suggests that Gene Forrester was on the limb with him. Gene looks to
Finny, who says that Gene was either on the ground or on the first rung
of the tree. Soon Gene realizes that he is being accused of Finny's accident.

Since no one can relate the details of the day exactly, the group wishes
that Leper were there because he could always remember exact details.
Finny mentions seeing Leper that day and two boys go to find him. In a
few minutes they return with Leper, who describes that one body was
out on the limb and another body was near the trunk of the tree. Then one
body moved and the other moved and then one body fell. When Brinker
asks Leper which body moved first, Leper declines to answer, saying that
he refuses to give out important informantion.

Phineas interrupts the proceedings by announcing that he doesn't
care and he begins to leave. Brinker asks him to wait until they get all the
facts. Phineas turns to Brinker and curses him and Gene notices that Finny
is crying. The next thing they hear is Finny's body "falling clumsily down
the white marble stairs."

Commentary

When Gene returns from having seen Leper, he "wanted to see Phineas, and Phineas only. With him there was no conflict except between athletes." But earlier Gene had thought there was a conflict between him and Finny. Now, however, since Finny has been wounded, he represents a world away from the adult conflicts and a world in which Gene is no longer involved with conflicts. It is now a safe world for Gene because there is no more rivalry. Ironically, however, Gene finds Finny involved in a snowball fight. This conflict, significantly, is a simple one, quite different from Leper's.

As Gene approaches the snowball fight, he is aware of the landscape, which he sees in terms of primeval innocence with the charming Finny "fighting and playing" amid groves of trees which suggest the untouched innocence of childhood. Gene concludes these images, saying "There is no such grove, I know now," and this is a realization from a later and more mature person. Returning to his adolescence, Gene sees himself as hesitating "on the edge of the fight and the edge of the woods, too tangled in my mind to enter either one or the other." In other words, Gene realizes his "tangled" predicament and he sees more now, or is aware of more meaning, than he was earlier in his life.

As Gene stands and watches Finny, he realizes that Finny acts with such authority only "when he had an idea which was particularly preposterous." Furthermore, Gene is now aware that Finny's coordination is not so perfect as it used to be. Gene is now maturing enough to evaluate Finny more objectively.

As Gene enters into the fight, he also observes Finny's actions, and records them as follows: "he turned his fire against me, he betrayed several of his other friends; he went over to the other, to Brinker's side for a short time, enough to ensure that his betrayal of them would heighten the disorder. Loyalties became hopelessly entangled." This evaluation is the first that Gene has ever been able to make of Finny's real nature. This description also catches Gene's essential problem with Finny. Gene has never been able to understand that Finny's life is based on disorder, on a violation of the rules and on spontaneous action. Gene could never change sides and still enjoy the battle, but Finny could do this. Thus, Finny's erratic actions cause loyalties to become hopelessly entangled, and as we look back on the earlier actions, we realize now that Finny's unpredictable actions caused Gene's loyalty to him to become so hopelessly entangled that he jounced the limb, causing Finny to fall in the same way that now the only method of ending the snowball fight is for everyone to turn against

Finny. But even with this action, note that Finny thought it "was a good fight.

Slowly, then, Gene is coming to a true understanding of his own and Finny's nature. The next scene shows part of Gene's change. He looks at some pictures that he had earlier implied were pictures of his own family place, but now, he is acquiring "a sense of [his] own real authority and worth" and no longer feels the need to lie about the pictures. Furthermore, when Brinker asks about Leper, Gene refuses to lie about the situation. He feels his "resentment against having to mislead people seemed to be growing stronger every day." Gene is now definitely maturing and developing some sense of integrity. This desire on his part can foreshadow the trial scene at the end of the chapter, where Brinker is also searching for the truth.

In contrast to Gene's desire to be honest with himself and honest about Leper, we see that he cannot be honest about Finny. When Brinker says that Finny is out of the war, Gene tries to deny it, but Finny admits that he is. This is a reversal on Finny's part and is typical of Finny's behavior. But Gene recognizes that if Finny is out of the war, it is because Gene is responsible. Gene is not ready to accept the dreadful responsibility of this act and thus tries to escape the consequences by assuming Finny's view that there is not a war. As soon as Finny admits that there is a war, Gene feels that the "facts were re-established, and gone were all the fantasies" of life. He is now back into reality and consequently, in terms of his development, we must have his trial to clear up all fantasies of the past.

In the days that follow, many recruiting officers come to the campus, and Gene feels that qualifying for their programs is quite peaceful compared to the qualifying that he had undergone the preceding summer for the Super Suicide Society. Now Gene begins to look upon adult life with more composure than he had faced the transition from adolescence. The relationship between the school and the recruiting officers was "as though Athens and Sparta were trying to establish not just a truce but an alliance — although we were not as civilized as Athens and they were not as brave as Sparta." In some sense, this analogy fits the relationship that has existed tween Gene and Finny — with Gene, of course, representing Athens and Finny standing for the more warlike Sparta. But after all the visits of the recruiting officers, Gene still takes no action because he didn't "feel free to." He is still on the edge, between the woods and the fight, or between adolescence and adulthood.

Brinker later accuses Gene of pitying Finny because Finny is now a cripple. Gene's strong resentment of Brinker's comments brings Brinker to question Gene about his role in Finny's accident. Brinker realizes that Finny was so natural as an athlete that it would have been highly unlikely for him to lose his balance. This realization, of course, accounts for Brinker's instigating the trial in a few days.

Before the trial, there is one final scene of special importance between Gene and Finny. Gene has been helping Finny translate some Latin which involves Caesar and a war, thus bringing back again the subject of war. This provides Finny with the rationale to tell Gene that he doesn't believe in the Gallic war and he continues by saying: "I don't believe books and I don't believe teachers...but I do believe—it's important after all for me to believe *you*." The irony here is that Gene is the person who has most betrayed Finny and yet Finny must believe in Gene. Like all adolescents, Finny must have someone whom he can completely trust. This trust accounts for Finny's refusal to believe that Gene could possibly betray him or could have jounced the limb. If Finny believed this, then there would be nothing in the world that he could trust. Consequently, he has completely closed his mind to the possibility that Gene acted in a manner contrary to friendship.

Finny explains further that he now must believe in the war because he has seen Leper himself and "if a war can drive somebody crazy, then it's real all right." When Finny comes out of his fantasies about the war, Gene emerges with him. They both then move from the dream world slowly into the real world, but their passage has only progressed far enough to allow them to react with all of the ramifications involved in the trial soon to follow. Even as they move out of their make-believe world, Gene admits that he liked Finny's world a lot better. Thus, we see one of the difficulties of facing the real world—it is not so much fun as a make-believe world.

The final scene of this chapter is the trial. Gene and Finny are taken to the assembly room in the First Building. It is a room which reminds Gene of death, and the other seniors in their black graduation robes add to the gloom and solemnity of the occasion. After Gene and Finny learn that the group is investigating Finny's accident, both are astonished and uncooperative. But gradually Finny begins to tell his story. When Brinker suggests to him that maybe he didn't "just fall out of that tree," Phineas suddenly becomes interested in the investigation. He has had the same feeling but has never pursued it. Throughout the investigation, we see that Finny is approaching the subject for the first time. In other words, as pointed out above, Finny must believe and trust Gene, and consequently has put out of his mind all suspicions that Gene had anything to do with the accident. Finny first becomes **suspicious** when Gene lies to the group about where he was standing. Finny does know that Gene was with him in the tree but he watches Gene lie to the group, saying that he was at the bottom of the tree.

As the investigation continues, Gene realizes that he is definitely being accused of causing Finny's accident. When the group sends for Leper, Gene feels that he will definitely be sentenced to guilt. It is ironic that Leper tells just enough for the group to be uncertain as to Gene's guilt, but the amount that Leper does tell is enough for Finny to finally realize that Gene did betray him in the tree. That is, Leper reports that one of the bodies in the tree jounced the limb. The group doesn't know which boy jounced the limb, but Finny and Gene do know.

At this point, Finny breaks from the room crying that he doesn't want to hear anymore. Finny maintains that he just doesn't want to know and doesn't care. In terms of what Finny has just told Gene in confidence, we realize that now that Finny knows of Gene's betrayal, there is nothing left for Finny to believe in. He leaves in utter desperation at the realization that he now can trust no one. This collapse of his inner values is represented by the sound of his body falling down the marble stairs.

CHAPTER 12

Summary

After Finny's fall, everyone behaves with perfect composure. One student remembers that the dispensary is not open; another goes directly to Dr. Stanpole's house. Meanwhile, Gene stands at the back of the gathered crowd watching Finny's reaction. He is afraid that his presence might disturb Phineas. When the doctor arrives, Gene hears him say that it is the same leg broken again.

After they carry Phineas away, Gene considers stealing a car; then realizes that such an act would be useless. He then thinks of the gym teacher, who tells everyone to "give it the old college try," and thinks probably that the teacher is now telling Finny to do the same. He wonders what is transpiring in the infirmary and he imagines the doctor and the "windbag nurse" gabbing to Phineas, and Finny will only answer them in Latin. At this and other thoughts, Gene begins to laugh; at least he thinks he is laughing until he puts his hand to his face and discovers that it is covered with tears.

Slowly, Gene works his way to the infirmary and finds Finny's room from the outside. After everyone is gone, he climbs up to the window and opens it from the outside. He calls to Finny and immediately Phineas asks him if he has come to "break something else." Finny tries to crawl out of bed threatening to get Gene, but instead, he only falls to the floor. Gene tries to apologize, but realizes that he is only causing more trouble for his friend. He leaves Finny to get back into bed by himself and then walks about the campus. He sleeps that night under the eaves of the gym.

The next morning, he sees a note pinned to his door. It is from the doctor, asking Gene to bring Finny's toilet articles and clothes to the infirmary. Gene dreads meeting Finny, and he slowly approaches the sick room. He finds Phineas sitting in bed leafing through a magazine. He tells Finny that he has brought his clothes. Finny examines the things very carefully; meanwhile, Gene feels a certain tension in the room. He cannot withstand the moment any longer, and he explains to Finny that he had tried to explain the entire accident last fall. Finny knows this and says only that he wishes there were no war. He tells Gene that he has tried to enlist and everyone has rejected him. That is why he has always pretended that there is no war. Gene explains to Finny that he could not be successful in the war, anyway, because he would get the sides and allegiances all mixed up.

Suddenly, Finny is crying and wondering why Gene pushed him out of the tree. He wants to think that it was a "blind impulse." He can't believe that it was "some kind of hate...it wasn't anything personal." Gene acknowledges that it wasn't, and Finny believes him.

Gene spends the remainder of the day attending classes and waiting for Dr. Stanpole to report on Finny's progress. At five P.M., Gene returns to hear the news on Finny's new cast and, the doctor tells him that Phineas is dead. The doctor explains that it was a simple fracture, but that some of the marrow must have gotten into the bloodstream. Gene can never cry over Finny's death because even when he was at the burial, he thought it was his own funeral, and one doesn't cry at one's own funeral.

Commentary

The images connected with Finny's lying on the stairs with his leg broken offer another reversal. He is seen as being "isolated at the center of a tight circle of faces." Previously, Phineas was always at the center of a circle, but never isolated. Now with the lack of trust destroyed by the revelation of Gene's guilt, Finny feels isolated from all people. As he had said previously, a person must believe in someone or else there is nothing. Furthermore, the images indicate a reversal in that Finny is now being carried and, by nature, Finny would usually be carrying someone else.

While Finny lies there, Gene has "the desolating sense of having all along ignored what was finest in" Finny. He begins to realize the extent to which he has been false to Finny. And he also realizes that as he had earlier wanted to be a part of Phineas, so Finny "had thought of [Gene] as an extension of himself."

After Finny is carried away, Gene thinks of stealing a car. This is a desire to escape from responsibility, but Gene represses this desire and remains to face his guilt. This is an act of maturity. Later in the night he is led to Finny's room and climbs up the outside window to peer in at Finny, but Phineas accuses Gene of coming to break something else. Gene realizes the extent to which he has injured Finny when he observes that Finny is "struggling to unleash his hate against me" and that he was unable to "because his matchless coordination was gone." Thus, Gene's acts have now completely immobilized the active and dynamic Phineas.

After Gene leaves Phineas, he wanders around the campus. He seemingly cannot return to his room, which he had previously shared with Finny. He returns to many of the places he and Finny had experienced in an attempt to see what meaning these places have for him alone.

When Gene goes to the infirmary to carry Finny's clothes and toilet things, he immediately observes an air of total indifference in Finny's behavior. He is neither friendly or unfriendly. For the first time, Finny is holding something back. He only wants to know why Gene came last night. Gene tries to explain that he thought he belonged there. In other words, Gene has not been able to reject the idea that he is a part of Finny.

Finny tries to bring the subject to the war. He wishes that the war did not exist. Again, Finny cannot tolerate the idea of conflict when he cannot participate in that conflict. For the first time, Gene tries to explain Finny's essential nature. He maintains that Finny would make a "terrible mess...out of the war." He remembers that in the snowball fight, Finny would change sides and confuse loyalties. The war with all its discipline and order would be a violation of Finny's essential nature.

When the subject of the accident comes up, Finny wants to believe Gene and suggests that Gene did it on a blind impulse. This is a rather accurate account of Gene's behavior. It again emphasizes a certain savage nature underneath a calm exterior. And Finny must believe Gene because otherwise Finny would have nothing to believe in.

Finny is killed by a particle of bone marrow entering the bloodstream and stopping his heart. Is his death necessary or has the author merely killed him off? The latter, of course, would be a major flaw in the novel. Finny's death, it seems, can be viewed as a natural sequence within the framework Knowles has constructed.

Finny's flowing unity, his vibrantly athletic response to life, has been crippled and maimed by two serious accidents. His leg, now broken, has been emphasized often in the novel as characterizing an athletic unity most essential to his vision of life. His body is of utmost importance to him. It is the source of his strength; he demands an utmost performance from it in sports. With this creative power for becoming effective gone, he cannot exist within his world.

In addition, Finny has structured an outer reality of boyhood glamor and of fantasy founded on whatever conflict he can conjure from the unexpected and foreseen. Crippled for life, and therefore, adjusting to crutches and wheelchairs, and to patronizing attitudes of others is impossible for Finny. His death, then, can be viewed as, structurally, correct. He is no longer the substance of throbbing life and can no longer function as a free-wheeling prep-school hero.

CHAPTER 13

Summary

In early June, Gene stands at the window and watches the war moving into the campus in the form of paratroopers with their regiment of sewing machines. Brinker wishes the Leper had joined this group because then he would not have "cracked up." Gene doesn't like to talk about something he can't change. He is thankful that no one has ever accused him "of being responsible for what had happened to Phineas."

Brinker takes Gene to meet Mr. Brinker, who thinks that the boys should enlist in a branch of the service which in later years reflect on their war record. He gives them a "speech about serving the country" which embarrasses both boys. Brinker is annoyed because he feels that his father's generation is responsible for the war that he and his friends have to fight. Gene, however, disagrees. He feels "that wars were made instead by something ignorant in the human heart."

Gene never talks about Phineas to anyone. He realizes that "Finny had a vitality which could not be quenched so suddenly, even by the marrow of his bone." And now Finny has escaped the war. But Gene never develops an intense level of "hatred for the enemy" because his war "ended before [he] ever put on a uniform." He understands that he "was on active duty all [his] time at school." He sees now that he "killed [his] enemy there."

Commentary

The last chapter presents Gene's evaluation of his past experiences. We hear that he was never accused "of being responsible for what had happened to Phineas" and that he never discussed Phineas because he could only discuss him in terms of the accident. Here, then, is Gene's final desire to be completely honest in his approach to Finny and to Finny's memory. But even though nothing was ever said about Finny, he was constantly present in Gene's mind. "Finny had a vitality which could not be quenched so suddenly," and Gene realized that he has accepted a part of Finny's view of life. That is, he now allows only facts which he can assimilate into his nature to be important. He rejects things which he cannot find a place for and in this way, he is now able to exist "without a sense of chaos and loss."

The appearance of Brinker's father emphasizes the difference between the adolescent's view of the war and the older generation's view. Gene does not feel that the older crowd "are responsible for it," instead he now knows that "wars were made instead by something ignorant in the human heart." Consequently, looking back, we now know that Gene created a war between himself and Finny which never existed. Furthermore, he cannot become enthusiastic over the Second World War because his own "war ended before" he ever put on a uniform. Gene concludes that he "killed my enemy there," meaning that he killed both Finny and also what was, at the same time, foreign and inadmissible to his way of life.

CHARACTER ANALYSIS

GENE FORRESTER (The Narrator)

Because the novel opens some fifteen years after the main events to be narrated, the first reaction of most readers is to look for what the recounting means to the narrator. In this case the narrator is Gene Forrester. He returns to the school campus where he spent his years as a student, particularly his sixteenth and seventeenth years. The narration of the events must then be seen as central and important events in the life of the narrator.

In his return to the campus, we see that Gene is interested in two things—the academic building (or First Building) and the tree which extends over the river. Thus, since he visits these places, we can begin to examine later events in terms of these two places. We later know that Gene's most traumatic experiences occurred in these places. With this information in hand, we are then prepared to examine more fully his basic nature, a nature which is best understood as one in opposition or in contrast to that possessed by Phineas. In other words, it is almost impossible to analyze the basic elements of Gene's personality without bringing in certain aspects of Phineas' nature.

Gene's life has always been one of conformity and obedience to rules and regulations. He has always devoted himself to fulfilling the demands made upon him by his superiors. He prefers to be in accord with rules and accepted behavior at all times. He is not the natural rebel who does things contrary to the dictates of society. Furthermore, he likes to be aware of all the possible implications in any situation before he acts. In general, he is not an individualist even though the person he most admires is an extreme individualist. It is easier for Gene to go with the crowd than it is for him to go against it. Consequently, he is constantly feeling trapped by Finny's active disregard for rules and Finny's impetuous behavior.

Gene is basically reserved by nature. He does not like to express directly his emotions. Finny is able to tell him what good friends they are, but Gene cannot bring himself to acknowledge this confession. Even with Leper, he likes to keep the relationship at a distance and is uncomfortable when Leper, discharged from the army, tries to tell Gene about the misfortunes encountered in the service.

With these qualities established, we then see that Gene feels the need to set up an ideal. He does so in the person of Finny, who represents everything that is opposite to Gene's nature. Gene then tries to emerge himself within the ideal and when he cannot do so, and when he realizes that there is no rivalry between him and Finny, he cannot stand his own self; thus he tries to destroy the ideal so that it can be brought down to his level. When he cripples Finny, then there is no more ideal and Gene is then able to devote himself to "making it up" to Finny for the terrible betrayal he committed.

Thus, Gene is the basic man of conformity who is dissatisfied with his life and tries to establish something more ideal. It is only much later in life that he is able to recognize that man must be himself and assimilate accordingly, and cannot measure himself by the abilities of another person.

PHINEAS (Finny)

Finny functions as the perfect ideal young man whose almost perfect nature arouses suspicion. He is the natural-born athlete who moves with perfect harmony, grace, and coordination. He has never been seen to make an awkward movement until he falls out of the tree. This clumsy accident is the first ungraceful action anyone has ever seen Finny make.

Finny is a person who responds to the immediate present. He delights in doing things which no one has ever thought of. Most of his actions are spontaneous and result from a momentary decision to do something. For example, it is a sudden inspiration to jump from the tree and it is an unpremeditated decision to go to the beach for the night. Finny, than, is the man of action who is not hampered by rules, conformity, or regulations.

Finny is also a person of reversals. He delights in setting up a situation where he is in complete control of everything, but at the same time, he is most delighted when something surprises him. He invents games which involve sudden reversals. He likes people who respond with "unregulated friendliness." He is delighted to be placed in a difficult position so as to see if he can talk his way out of it.

Action with Finny is paramount. He does not think of the consequences or of the problems involved in any action. He acts, then, often without thinking. He breaks the school record, but his performance is important only to himself. He will not repeat the same performance for the benefit of an official timekeeper. In other words, he is content with himself as judge or timekeeper.

Finny responds to things and people with the same degree of spontaneity and warmth. He is not afraid to express openly his emotions or his feelings to anyone. This is because he is perfectly sure of himself and never fears making a blunder or mistake. He trusts other people with the same degree of faith that he himself expects to be trusted. Consequently, he feels ashamed of himself when he even thinks momentarily that Gene is responsible for his fall from the tree.

In general, Finny is the perfectly natural and spontaneous person who is not capable of doing something mean or ugly. He responds to life with natural emotions and all things, except studying, come easily to him. He is not capable of such emotions as jealousy or envy. He lives in a world of happiness and joy and he communicates these qualities to the people whom he meets.

LEPER (Edwin Lepellier)

Leper serves as a contrast to both Gene and Finny. He is the student who seems self-absorbed in his own affairs. He would have been an unobjectionable citizen of America had the war not come along. He functions in his own private world, but when the war called him forth to function in another type of world, he becomes "psycho" and must be discharged from the service for medical reasons.

In contrast to Finny, Leper represents the segment of the world which is not interested in everyday activities. The discovery of a beaver dam is more important than the war or than any sport victory. In contrast to Gene, Leper lives an unregulated life. He is totally wrapped up in his own pursuit of beavers and butterflies, so that when he must convert to a life of conformity and regulations such as is demanded by the army, Leper becomes the psychotic individual.

BRINKER HADLEY

Brinker plays a minor role in the novel, but nonetheless an important one. He stands for the average class leader. He is the organizer and the class representative. As such, he feels the need to be the guardian of the class's record. Consequently, since there is a war, he senses personally Leper's "crack up" and feels that Finny's accident must be investigated, so that there will be no more casualties from the class than necessary.

MOTIFS

THE SONG MOTIF

When Gene and Finny return from leaping out of the "forbidden" tree, they hear, from a long way off, background music of a loud phonograph accompanying their walk to the dormitory. It seems that the four songs which the boys hear might be noted by the reader as motifs to watch developing during the novel.

"Don't Sit Under the Apple Tree" echoes what Gene has just been persuaded to do. The tree, from which he leaps, becomes a genesis for self-knowledge, and although the apple tree is not implicitly Eden's fruit tree, it is accepted popularly as the "forbidden fruit." Gene, thus, has laid down his Virgil in the grass, climbed the tree and, defying authority, leaped into the unknown.

The song "They're Either Too Young or Too Old" suggests the extremes of age lying on either side of the magical, mythical peace of adolescence. Gene characterizes adolescence as "a sign of the life the war" is being fought to preserve. This age span of adolescence then is very special, and Knowles carefully describes the Devon's peacelike setting and the special, separate attitudes and emotions, as distinct from the "too old" and "too young," which unify and bind the boys together.

"The Warsaw Concerto" announces the awareness of the boys that World War II has begun. More important, the music accompanies the internal war Gene will be waging with Finny and with himself.

"The Nutcracker Suite" concerns Leper's insanity, his breakdown, the so-called psycho actions of Gene, which he recognizes as, colloquially, "nutty." It is on the heels of Gene's appraisal of Leper and of himself that he gains mature stature.

THE EDEN MOTIF

Chapters 1-5 contain an abundance of pastoral, Eden-like images and descriptive passages. This section of the book can be seen as picturing a peaceful, summer session at a New England boy's school. The peace, however, is mythic because, as Gene the narrator, comments "...there are few relationships among us at Devon not based on rivalry." The headmasters of the school and the parents of the boys, however, insist on maintaining a belief in this "separate peace" of adolescent boys. The green lushness of the summer enhances the idyllic tendency of the oldster's imagination, and it is during the summer that the author's flashback begins.

"We were still calmly, numbly reading Virgil and playing tag in the river farther downstream. Until Finny thought of the tree."

Here is the on-the-surface, undisturbed peace until the discordant element of Finny enters and suggests challenging the tree. The tree leads to Gene's eventual self-examination and self-knowledge, but only after many chapters of frustration, doubt, and, finally, savage violence. The reader should be aware that Finny does not represent Evil or a Snake. Finny's difference from the other boys is a healthy, wild, outdoor magnetism. The evil attributed to Finny festers within Gene's confusion of love and hate, loyalty, emulation, and deception of Finny.

The school is described in terms of its — "...enormous playing fields ....healthy green turf...brushed with dew...faint green haze...cricket noises...bird cries....expansive tops to all the elms....rustling early summer movement of the wind...." Over the lush naturalness of Devon reigns the symbol of the school's authority — the bell: "...matriarchial... the calmest, most carrying bell toll in the world, civilized, calm, invincible, and final.... [sounding] ten stately times." Tradition, as authoritarian as a tolling bell, then, rules Devon. Tradition here extends to tradition of ways of acting, and, more important, traditional ways of thinking.

There is everywhere a "...clean-washed shine of summer mornings. ...clear June days...thick layers of ivy, old-looking leaves you would have thought stayed there winter and summer, permanent hanging gardens.... umbrellas of leaves...a world of branches with an infinity of leaves... permanent and never-changing, an untouched, unreachable world high in space...."

This is in contrast to the variations of change of an adolescent into manhood. Manhood, Gene's, comes only after a knowledge and challenge to his integrity.

Knowles notes "...the Devon Woods, trees reached in an unbroken, widening corridor so far to the north that no one had ever seen the other end....the last and greatest wilderness."

He says, in effect, that the element of wildness, of wilderness, is present too in this green Eden of seeming peace. The wild element he refers to exists in the inner battles between the phases of adolescenthood in which values become individualized through conflict and confrontation.

"...one summer day after another broke with a cool effulgence over us, and there was a breath of widening life in the morning air — ...an oxygen intoxicant.... these mornings were too full of beauty for me, because I knew of too much hate to be contained in a world like this."

Gene's hate is a confusion of love and hate, both for himself and for Finny. Gene is in a static peace in this ordered pastoral setting of Devon until Finny challenges Gene's conservative personality with a vibrant, unbridled and responsive approach to living. Finny's living is made, of course, of exaggerated gestures, but exaggeration is necessary to jar tradition-bound thinking and acting.

Chapter 6 abruptly begins: "Peace had deserted Devon," referring generally to the peace of Gene's unexamined life. After Gene's leap from the tree, and after Gene causes Finny to fall, both falls (since Gene's first

58

leap was more a fall in fear than a jump in jest anyway) from (perhaps, symbolically) the Tree of Knowledge (for Gene), the book chronicles Gene's search for exact and individual standards.

QUESTIONS

1. Write an imaginative essay suggesting some of the possible meanings attached to the tree.

2. What is Leper's function in the novel?

3. What is gained symbolically by having two different rivers?

4. Show how Gene's personality is the direct opposite of Finny's.

5. Why is the trial at the end of the novel necessary?

6. Defend the necessity of Finny's death.

7. What is the purpose of Leper's "crack-up?"

8. How does World War II function as an important event throughout the novel?

9. Is Gene's act of jouncing the limb a rational or an irrational act? Defend your choice.

10. Contrast Brinker's changing adolescence with that of Gene's.

Your Guides to Successful Test Preparation.

Cliffs Test Preparation Guides
• Complete • Concise • Functional • In-depth

Efficient preparation means better test scores. Go with the experts and use *Cliffs Test Preparation Guides*. They focus on helping you know what to expect from each test, and their test-taking techniques have been proven in classroom programs nationwide. Recommended for individual use or as a part of a formal test preparation program.

Publisher's ISBN Prefix 0-8220

Qty.	ISBN	Title	Price	Qty.	ISBN	Title	Price
	2078-5	ACT	8.95		2044-0	Police Sergeant Exam	9.95
	2069-6	CBEST	8.95		2047-5	Police Officer Exam	14.95
	2056-4	CLAST	9.95		2049-1	Police Management Exam	17.95
	2071-8	ELM Review	8.95		2076-9	Praxis I: PPST	9.95
	2077-7	GED	11.95		2017-3	Praxis II: NTE Core Battery	14.95
	2061-0	GMAT	9.95		2074-2	SAT*	9.95
	2073-4	GRE	9.95		2325-3	SAT II*	14.95
	2066-1	LSAT	9.95		2072-6	TASP	8.95
	2046-7	MAT	12.95		2079-3	TOEFL w/cassettes	29.95
	2033-5	Math Review	8.95		2080-7	TOEFL Adv. Prac. (w/cass.)	24.95
	2048-3	MSAT	24.95		2034-3	Verbal Review	7.95
	2020-3	Memory Power for Exams	5.95		2043-2	Writing Proficiency Exam	8.95

Prices subject to change without notice.

Available at your booksellers, or send this form with your check or money order to **Cliffs Notes, Inc., P.O. Box 80728, Lincoln, NE 68501 http://www.cliffs.com**

☐ Money order   ☐ Check payable to Cliffs Notes, Inc.

☐ Visa ☐ Mastercard   Signature_____

Card no. _____ Exp. date_____

Signature _____

Name _____

Address _____

City _____ State_____ Zip_____

*GRE, MSAT, Praxis PPST, NTE, TOEFL and Adv. Practice are registered trademarks of ETS. SAT is a registered trademark of CEEB.

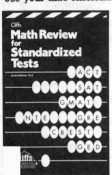

Study Smart with Cliffs StudyWare®

Think Quick...Again

Now there are more Cliffs Quick Review® titles, providing help with more introductory level courses. Use Quick Reviews to increase your understanding of fundamental principles in a given subject, as well as to prepare for quizzes, midterms and finals.

Think quick with new Cliffs Quick Review titles. You'll find them at your bookstore or by returning the attached order form. Do better in the classroom, and on papers and tests with Cliffs Quick Reviews.

Cliffs® NOTES INC.